Brooching
It
Diplomatically

A TRIBUTE TO MADELEINE K. ALBRIGHT

ARNOLDSCHE
Art Publishers

EXHIBITION TOUR

Helen Drutt: Philadelphia,
Philadelphia, PA, USA
September 10 – September 26, 1998

Museum Het Kruithuis,
's-Hertogenbosch, The Netherlands
October 10 – November 15, 1998

Taideteollisuusmuseo,
Helsinki, Finland
December 3, 1998 – February 7, 1999

Tarbekunstimuuseum,
Tallinn, Estonia
February 27 – April 4, 1999

Museum voor Moderne Kunst,
Oostende, Belgium
April 16 – May 23, 1999

American Craft Museum,
New York, New York, USA
June 3 – August 8, 1999

The Contemporary Museum,
Honolulu, Hawaii, USA
September 3, 1999 – November 7,1999

Philadelphia International Airport,
Philadelphia, Pennsylvania, USA
December 23, 1999 – April 30, 2000

Villa Croce,
Museum of Contemporary Art,
Genoa, Italy
June 14 – July 30, 2000

Kunstgewerbemuseum,
Berlin, Germany
August 27 – November 25, 2000

Schmuckmuseum,
Pforzheim, Germany
December 9, 2000 – February 11, 2001

This catalogue is published on the occasion of
the exhibition "Brooching It Diplomatically"
by Helen Drutt: Philadelphia, with support
from the Museum of Art and Design, Helsinki,
Finland and the Museum Het Kruithuis,
's-Hertogenbosch, The Netherlands.

Copyright 1998
HELEN DRUTT: PHILADELPHIA
1721 Walnut Street, Philadelphia,
PA 19103, USA
Postal Address: 2222 Rittenhouse Square,
Philadelphia, PA 19103-5505, USA
Website: http://www.libertynet.org/~druttphl/
and artists

English-German edition published by:
ARNOLDSCHE ART PUBLISHERS
Liststraße 9, D-70178 Stuttgart
Tel: +49/711/61 24 60, Fax: +49/711/ 615 98 43
Website: http://www.arnoldsche.com
e-Mail: art@arnoldsche.com

Die Deutsche Bibliothek
CIP-Einheitsaufnahme
Ein Titeldatensatz für diese Publikation ist
bei der Deutschen Bibliothek erhältlich
ISBN 3-89790-152-8

Photo Credits:
Rien Bazen: 27; Thomas Brummett: 37, 41, 99;
Tom van Eyende: 29; Timothy Greenfield-
Sanders: Portrait of Madeleine K. Albright; David
Cripps: 93; Joseph Painter: 43, 79, 119; Jack
Ramsdale: 25, 31, 34, 35, 39, 45, 51, 52, 53, 55,
57, 59, 65, 69, 70, 71, 73, 75, 83, 85, 89, 94-95,
105, 107, 109, 113, 115, 121, 122, 123, 127,
128, 129, 131, 135, 137, 139, 141, 143; Rauno
Träskelin: 61.

Contents

The publishers wish to express their
appreciation to Helen Drutt in
Philadelphia for her cooperation and
helpfulness at all time.

Introduction

"If I were asked...to what the singular prosperity and growing strength of that people (Americans) ought mainly to be attributed, I should reply: to the superiority of their women."

- Alexis De Tocqueville

"One is not born a woman, one becomes one."

- Simone De Beauvoir
  The Second Sex

Eagles, a top hat, snakes, bees, balloons, spiders, and the Capitol Building leaped off the page from under a headline: "Brooching it Diplomatically." It was an article in *Time Magazine*, March 27, 1997, about an unusual strategy on the part of Madeleine K. Albright, the first woman in American history to hold the position of Secretary of State. Mrs. Albright, it turns out, announces her views through the brooches she chooses to wear and the article surveyed the variety of messages she was sending. Sparks flew as I thought of the artists who could respond, if challenged, to an invitation to create an unique brooch for a woman in her position.

The idea was born, and then the research began. Communicating with artists throughout the world, not to mention the Department of State, was a complex challenge. A letter was posted to the Secretary of State expressing my desire to organize an invitational exhibition in tribute to her recognition of the power of brooches, and in the months to come, her office was kept fully informed of the developments. In the eighteen months since the *Time* article appeared, seventy-four invitations were mailed, and sixty-one artists from sixteen countries responded with seventy-one works remarkable for their creativity and inventiveness, as well as their humor, irony and patriotism. Nine brooches were not created specifically for this project, but were pieces the artists felt were appropriate to the theme. All illuminate the credibility of the ornament as historical commentary.

Jewelry is the most personal of art forms and its intimate connection with human beings is inescapable. The works of art in this exhibition are meant to be worn (not hidden in a drawer or velvet box) as a symbol of position, a badge of honor, a mark of ritual experience or for pure pageantry. They form a visual connection between the artist, the wearer and the audience which establishes an intellectual identity. In the case of Madeleine K. Albright, that identification is magnified across an international public forum. Knowing that she is in a position of power, she puts her sensibilities to the test. She obviously trusts her instincts and has the confidence to herald her negotiating stand to the whole world with her brooches.

George Magazine has noted that a liberty eagle perched on a faux pearl has become the "brooch of security" in political and diplomatic circles in Washington, D.C. It is our wish that this exhibition sings out "Bye Bye Birdie" to the safety pin. Here we are taking our cue from Madame Secretary herself, who stated in *Newsweek* (November 5, 1997): "If we want our views and interests respected, we cannot sit on the sidelines..." Likewise, we cannot allow the gold-plated, cast eagle to fly unchallenged when there are flocks of artists full of creative ideas:
• Laurie Hall's piece *Cutting* emblazons "conscience" on a pair of silver scissors to urge a "sensitive regard to fairness and justice"; a simple *VIP* by Ramona Solberg salutes the distinction of Madeleine K. Albright; and Nancy Worden's *Arms*

Agreement is a visual reminder that Mrs. Albright's handshakes are "gestures of courtesy and good will."

• Merrily Tompkins' brooch makes a plea for the Secretary of State to use her position to deplore the practice of female genital mutilation, whereas Louis Mueller hopes that *Subscribe*, taken from *ARTFORUM*, will remind the world to support the arts.

• Esther Knobel's *Kisses from Jerusalem* look like miniature fire bombs disguised as Hershey Kisses which comprise a set of ambiguous ornaments. They are in complete contrast to the classic form of Yasuki Hiramatsu's gold brooch which represents the harmony of five continents on earth and his wish for world peace.

• Descended from Chinese grandparents, Ron Ho allows his ancestry to symbolize Madeleine K. Albright's presence and position in the form of a dragon, which "represents power and wisdom."

• Karel Votipka's postmodern brooch construction celebrates an American skyscraper with two adjoining towers representing our neighbors Mexico and Canada. Other constructions include Thomas Gentille's aluminum square, precise in the purity of its form, Peter de Wit's replica of the *Washington Monument* made of crystal and precious gems, and Barbara Seidenath's geometric form inlaid with diamonds.

• Daniel Jocz's narrative *Punch* in gold relief suggests the diplomatic exchange of verbal blows. Bettina Speckner uses photographs taken by her mother when she first visited America, which evokes Mrs. Albright's journeys to other lands. Hilde De Decker's casts gold coins of various countries hang from a branch as if they were cherries waiting to be plucked as the Secretary of State enters each domain.

• While looking at the ocean, Sondra Sherman thought that gold fragments shaped like the continents could drift in water and remind us that the "globe is a large gem"; this thought led to *Continental Drift*. Richard Mawdsley's petrified insect-like tower is a counterpoint to Margareth Sandström's golden angel, which could graciously adorn the Secretary of State on any occasion. Tore Svensson hopes that she will find the opportunity to wear one of his quartet of brooches whose designs were based on mourning cloths woven by Paracas Indians of Peru.

No exhibition can occur without the assistance of a community. This exhibition and catalogue have been achieved through the efforts of many individuals. The enthusiastic response of the artists made the initial concept a reality and their support is deeply appreciated. For their assistance in collating research material, I would like to thank Martha Flood, the keeper of our archives, Alexandra Kudrjav-cev-DeMilner for her assistance in establishing the biographical format in the midst of another project, and Brenda Moore, my gallery assistant, who lent immeasurable assistance in the final stages of the project. Jack Ramsdale provided the photographic documentation with additional assistance from Thomas Brummett and Joseph Painter. A special thank you to Michael Lemonick of *Time Magazine*, who provided the link which located Timothy Greenfield-Sanders and made it possible for us to publish his distinguished portrait of Madeleine K. Albright. Peter Grollman, an assistant to U.S. Senator Arlen Specter, served as an enthusiastic liaison between this project and the Department of State. Wendy Steiner, whose current work deals with women, ornament, and beauty, was delighted to contribute an essay which explores the role that ornament can play in the life of a powerful woman.

Yvònne Joris, Director of the Museum Het Kruithuis, 's-Hertogenbosch, The Netherlands acted as a catalyst in bringing the exhibition to Europe. In addition her institution prepared the works for an international tour. Marianne Aav, Director of Exhibitions at the Museum of Art and Design in Helsinki, Finland oversaw the catalogue design and printing in Finland. Her institution supported this publication through its contribution to the design and by lending its resources throughout the stages of catalogue production. A special thank you goes to Gijs Bakker who selected a designer, Jari Silvennoinen, whose efforts and vision produced a document worthy of the person to whom this tribute is being paid. We realized McLuhan's prophecy of a global village by our interaction via fax, telephone, and postal express which proved, indeed, to be lifesaving.

In 1906 René Lalique created an olive branch brooch with eight birds initially described as pigeons. After the original Armistice Day in 1918, the "pigeons" made a significant transition into doves of peace as the ornament became a symbolic gift from the citizens of Paris to Mrs. Woodrow Wilson. Unfortunately, the sentiments behind this well-meaning peace symbol failed, for Congress rejected U.S. entry into the League of Nations, thus making it impossible to implement its objectives. We can only hope that the symbols worn by Madeleine Albright will not fail, but assist her in realizing world harmony as she reaches out to governments of all nations. *Brooching It Diplomatically* supports the reality that artists' jewelry can go beyond the limits of ornament to satisfy greater aesthetic and political needs. In doing so, this exhibition celebrates our Secretary of State's honored position as her image merges creative and diplomatic expression.

HELEN W. DRUTT ENGLISH

Founder/Director
Helen Drutt: Philadelphia
September 1998

T his exhibition began with a simple invitation. "Dear Artist," wrote Helen
W. Drutt English, "shall we 'brooch' (broach) the subject diplomatically?"
The subject in question was Madeleine K. Albright, the first woman to be named
Secretary of State in American history, and the pun on "brooch" was more apt
than the letter-writer could know. For "brooch" and "broach" are the same
word, according to the *Oxford English Dictionary*, with two senses only recently
differentiated through spelling. "Brooch" comes from a verb meaning to stab,
pierce into in order to liberate something, tap, give vent or publicity to, begin
conversation or discussion about, introduce, moot. Etymologically speaking,
brooches do broach.

Secretary Albright has employed this semantic coincidence to her diplomatic advantage. Ever since ascending to the highest Cabinet post, she has used
her brooches to express the aims of her negotiations. A dove gleamed off her
shoulder in recent Middle-East peace talks, telegraphed over the wire services to
observers across the world. Because this vehicle for symbolism has not been
used by male diplomats, Mrs. Albright's jeweled broaching has provoked a
public discussion about the relation between femininity and power. Time,
Vogue, George, and other Albright-watchers have documented the ornamental
semiotics invented by the Secretary of State. She wears a jeweled spider when
she feels alluring, a Capitol brooch to show her bipartisanship, a balloon pin
when she is feeling up.[i] By wearing her bee brooch, she appropriates

Mohammad Ali's advice to "float like a butterfly, sting like a bee." She has chosen the bee, not the butterfly – a message not lost on her negotiating partners – but she does so by a means available only to a woman. Like Ophelia's language of flowers, the language of brooches expresses the mental state of the Secretary of State. "Read my pins,"[ii] she quips.

Secretary Albright's brooches have sometimes revealed a tug-of-war between the meanings others give her and those she chooses for herself. After the Iraqi press called her a serpent, she wore a snake brooch to meet with Tariq Aziz. When Ratko Mladic named a goat after her, a U.S. admiral presented her with a goat pin. His diplomatic gallantry, like the snake brooch flaunted in Aziz's presence, transformed an insult into a compliment. As in Shakespeare's *Tempest*, where jeweled art redeems death – "Those are pearls that were his eyes. Look!" – here brooches redeem aggression, turning it back onto the aggressor. Mrs. Albright and the admiral show not only that it isn't nice to insult a lady, but that you shoot yourself in the foot by doing so. 'Those are pearls that were his snub. Look!'

Of course, artists throughout time have designed jewelry for powerful women – empresses, queens, heiresses, celebrities. But whether it was the Crown Jewels of England or Fouquet's Art Nouveau breastplates for Sarah Bernhardt, the traditional functions of ornament have supported the alliance between femininity and power. The costliness of precious materials proves the prestige of the wearer, and the beauty of design and workmanship enhances her attractiveness. Though women monarchs have always had a complicated path to negotiate in exerting political power, the arts of display have at least been their allies. And for celebrities and actresses such as Sarah Bernhardt, the mystique created by ornament has increased their power on the stage and in the public imagination.

However, female power-brokers in a democracy, and particularly a post-feminist democracy, cannot so blithely advertise their beauty, allure, wealth, and personal taste. On the contrary, democratic power must appear to be diffused rather than concentrated in one over-determined center. As a result, in no major American city is female dress as conservative as in Washington, where lacquered bouffant hair-dos are known as "power helmets," and dressing for success for a woman means wearing fire-engine-red suits with gilt buttons. Washington jewelry expresses approved values, such as patriotism and restrained tastefulness, and it is safest if it comes in copies that "everyone" is wearing, for example, the "liberty eagle" recently worn by virtually every First Lady and female politician in the country. Capitol style is a matter of control and conformity, not self-expression. Though women are not supposed to hide their femininity in a male imitation, neither are they supposed to express it in a female-aristocratic message inconsistent with democratic power--as capriciousness, willfulness, allure, narcissism, irresistible fascination. Of course, some Washington women convey all these messages about female power, but a Secretary of State might find it problematic to do so. As the news coverage surrounding Mrs. Albright suggests, a detente between her femininity and power is under continuous negotiation.

The brooches in this exhibition reflect this ideological complexity, and in doing so, reveal perennial tensions at work in jewelry. Is the aim of a brooch to enhance the appearance of the wearer or to stand independently as a work of art in its own right? If a brooch conveys a political message from the artist, is it proper for a public figure to lend out her body to transmit it? If wearing it means that she subscribes to the brooch's message, what insight does the artist have into the messages she might care to communicate? Is it appropriate for a public figure to use ornament in a conventionally feminine fashion to express her own taste or the desire to please through her appearance? Or must she eschew personal messages, never neglecting any avenue to express the dignity of her position and the aims of the particular mission she is on?

The answers to these questions are as varied as the artists in this exhibition. Some have chosen to ignore Mrs. Albright's gender (except insofar as the brooch is nowadays conventionally a feminine ornament). Free then to communicate purely diplomatic ideas, Kai Chan's *Mountains & Seas* expresses a reciprocity between Canada and the United States, its red mountains mirroring the blue waves across the "border" between them. Margaret West's *Cloud Rose* in white translucent marble captures an Australian sublimity of nature; her countryman, Robert Baines, turns kangaroos into whimsical design elements in his red filigreed *Oz Brooch*. Jiří Šibor and Pavel Opočenský carve U.S. symbols in decorative stone: èibor's relief map of the States wrought in coral, with a separate coral pins for Alaska and Hawaii, and Opočenský's rendering in polished jade of the American flag, with its edge left rough as if the flag were billowing in the wind. These nationalistic symbols--earnest, lyrical, or humorous--put little pressure on the Secretary of State either as a woman or a diplomat. They accept the idea of the stateswoman as nonproblematic.

Wendy Ramshaw's and Juhani Heikkilä's pieces go even further in this gender-obliviousness. Ramshaw's *Lightning*, an electricity bolt in silver, gold, and semi-precious stones, expresses power and mental energy. "I think this is an appropriate piece for somebody who must depend upon logic and flashes of perception," Ramshaw writes in a letter to Helen Drutt.[iii] "'Lightning' could also act as a conductor and conduit for rational lateral thinking. It is the expression of a moment of energy."[iv] Heikkilä's *Brooch* provides what amounts to a rationale for ignoring the sex of a leading official. It is a male nude with a rod extended outward as an arm labeled "homo communicans." Just as Latin is (or once was for Europe) a universal, international language, "homo" is the generic "person" – male, like this nude, only by convention. The Secretary of State's essence is to be a communicator, and for Heikkilä this diplomatic function is independent of her sex. Both Ramshaw and Heikkilä posit a post-sexist world in which jobs are done by people with the non-gender-specific attributes to do them well: in this case, energy, logic, perception, and skill in communication.

But even when artists cannot ignore Mrs. Albright's sex, they often do not present it as having any particular effect on her role as the head of U.S. foreign policy. Kiff Slemmons's brooch looks like a lorgnette with two "lenses" that resemble ship's compasses. One contains the figure of a woman with a flowing gown and the other, the surrounding silver left when the figure was cut out of the plate: the woman present, the woman absent. Mrs. Albright travels a lot, and the U.S. inscription "In God We Trust" conveys the idea that sometimes she is in the States and at other times she is away. The compasses are joined by a plexiglas rod finished with a fine pen nib. This brooch relates femininity, the official signature, navigation, and travel in a formally elegant design.

Many of the artists in this exhibition have appropriated the Statue of Liberty, a readymade representation of the United States as female. Marjorie Schick's *Liberty Torch* redoes the famous symbol as a bouquet of papier-mâché flower-flames. Betsy King uses the Statue in her *World Peace*, which may be a pun on the brooch itself, a "world piece." The brilliant Gijs Bakker casts a steel outline of Lady Liberty's head and inserts watches for the eyes: "One upside down for Mrs. Albright to know how long her appointment will last and her visitor at what time to leave."[v] Bakker's brooch is thus an aid for the practical Mrs. Albright. With similar considerateness, Gerd Rothmann's brooch provides her with a handy presentation piece for distinguished visitors. It is a gold plaque with the Secretary's thumbprint and the inscription "With Honor and Gratitude, Presented by the Secretary of State Madeleine K. Albright." The brooch comes in a fitted box with a space left for filling in the recipient's identity.

Some artists ignore Mrs. Albright altogether in their eagerness to express ideological messages. After all, how often do you get to hang your beliefs on the shoulder of a U.S. Secretary of State? *Pentagon-Windmill* by the Dutch artist Robert Smit is an exquisite piece of goldsmithing, but at the same time hints that the Pentagon's swords should be melted into the Dutch equivalent of "ploughshares," windmills. The Swiss Bernhard Schobinger crosses rusted keys over a prison lock, conveying the oppressiveness of political power. The African-American artist Joyce Scott beads a Black Power fist over a map of Africa with a red, white, and blue South Africa, and calls it *Liberty*. And the Australian-French Pierre Cavalan creates collaged "decorations" that look like military medals: a boomerang held by a Black Power fist chained to the image of an Australian aborigine in a loincloth. This image is on a souvenir pin of the city of Darwin, but the name belongs to the evolutionary biologist as well, and implies that there has been little development from the situation of the spear-carrying "native" to that of the revolutionary African-American. For Cavalan, the two countries have much in common, perhaps not to their credit.

The polemics of other brooches concern not only politics but art. The exquisite workmanship of the German, Manfred Bischoff, produces a surreal vision of class in *Workingman Hero*. Here a skull "pushes" a wheelbarrow filled with its headless body, a weapon raised in triumph in the body's iron fist. In this absurdist allegory, the victory of the laborer is also his undoing, and this idea is itself transmitted through the intricate labor of a master goldsmith. More openly about the ideology of art, Stephan Seyffert's gold brick has the words, ARTICLE OF VALUE, inscribed upon it. Is it merely the material of the goldsmith's art – gold, in this case – that is valuable, or is it what the artist does with the material – shaping it into a symbol of that material, the gold brick? Or are we to read this brooch as a pun on "article of faith" or even "Articles of the Constitution," now replaced in U.S. diplomacy by a purely commercial "article"? The Israeli Deganit Schocken is more optimistic about the relations between art and politics. She places raised green trees, a sunken lake, and a border-crossing barrier in a balanced composition to suggest that "Disjunctive elements find their home in relation to one another as they merge in one geography. Integrity depends on a response that is prepared to strain for harmony, beauty and peace. We share olive trees and sand in the Middle East. We must reconcile our differences."

For other artists, however, the possibility of transmitting messages in jewelry is not so clear. Beppe Kessler's two brooches are decorative abstractions of plexi, fabric, paint, and newsprint with a round magnifying glass embedded in each. By looking through the glass bubbles we can read snatches of a message: "most inspired by the observed [obscene?] local..." and "-d a chance/ want to say/ -ns on whatever/ about/ It is good/ bad." However we might strain, this message is difficult to decipher--a secret (diplomatic? personal?) located behind a precious surface.

A number of works in this exhibition supply Mrs. Albright with exquisite ornamental art. The geometric elegance of Peter Skubic's designs in gleaming gold bespeak luxury, tastefulness, and aesthetic depth. Skubic reminds us that the Greek word "Kosmos" meant not only "order" and "space," but also ornament, jewelry. "My philosophy is to find the relationship between these different meanings," he writes.[vi] Breon O'Casey's golden dove flies within a silver, sun-dotted frame, a composition suggesting the Celtic symbolism of O'Casey's adopted Cornwall and the easy congress between landscape and abstraction among St. Ives artists. In the final works of the late Max Fröhlich made for this exhibition, gold wires coil over golden squares. "I wonder what you are thinking of the idea of the symbol of spirals for a high person of her standard?" he asked Helen Drutt in a letter. In another delicate work, Lucy Sarneel's *See-Ear* packs a hinged zinc box with a brooch of zinc plant forms. One opens the lid as if looking underwater to glimpse the teeming life on an ocean floor. Another harmony of jewelry and container is Catherine Martin's gold arabesque with its handmade box. William Harper's *Shiva's Golden Shaft*, Helen Shirk's sea anemones, Arline Fisch's *Ruffled Banner*, Debra Rapoport's *Grace*, and Detlef Thomas's *Malachite* are other works that speak the purest language of ornament, augmenting the attraction and prestige of the wearer through their condensed beauty.

Though many of these brooches talk politics or express femininity, a number adjust the idea of femininity through politics. Among the most elegant of these are Georg Dobler's two translations of the male diplomat's boutonniere into their perfect feminine analogues: the exquisite amethyst-and-silver and amethyst-and-gold flower pins. With them, the adjective "debonnaire" becomes a woman's word. Ruudt Peters's *David* also manages to merge male and female in attaching an "aerial" of technological wire to a natural jade crystal. Peters imagines Mrs. Albright wearing this brooch in talks with Prime-Minister Netanyahu, and one wonders, in that case, which way the symbolism will go. Will Israel play the youthful David to the mega-might of America's Goliath, or is it the female Secretary of State who must marshall her courage before the bellicose Prime-Minister?

Several jewelers see a special value for femininity in politics. Joan Binkley's silver-beaded brooch resembles a Medusa-haired mirror on a scorpion-tail "handle," an amalgam of traditional signs of the narcissism and the menace of Woman. Binkley has also tucked a steel peace symbol into the beaded elements at the bottom of the pin (elements that echo the inside of the peace symbol), as if Binkley were implying that beauty, femininity, and fetish should be deployed in the cause of peace. Similarly, Sharon Church's *Speak Softly* and *Scatter Pins* use the images of female fecundity and generosity (the bursting seed pod, the hand dropping fruit) to demonstrate the good that can come of a woman with power. Her title *Speak Softly* alludes to the political dictum, "Speak softly and carry a big stick." And Karl Fritsch's pin is a tiny, black pussycat adorned with two gold balls (breasts? the beads of a necklace?). The sweetness and miniaturization of this image convey Fritsch's anti-monumental politics, a protest against the idealizing sublimity and aggressive scale of German art that he associates with the rise of Nazism.[vii] The tiny female cat deploys power by undermining it, in a "strategy of democratization."

Among these "takes" on feminine statecraft, humor and irony abound. Peter Chang provides a Federalist mirror with duck's feet – because "a duck could be somebody's mother"? Sandra Enterline lays out a real "queen bee" in a gold casket. Judy Onofrio parodies a military medal by assembling found "jewels" around a kitsch bust of a deer wearing green mascara and crimson lipstick. Circling the deer's head are a keychain pendant with a view of Mt. Rushmore, a rhinestone American eagle, and a sparkling American Flag: All Bright for Madeleine? Bruce Metcalf's little golden man with a maple leaf for a head and a tiny penis between his legs holds out a wooden box of maple seeds. It is hard to imagine what it would mean for a female Secretary of State to wear such a brooch, especially since, as Metcalf states, "the human body is probably the most intimate and subversive arena for artworks."[viii] But considering the wit of this exquisite cartoon, wearing it might simply mean that Mrs. Albright had a sense of humor.

Betsy King's *Earth Angel* presents an array of female images that Mrs. Albright might encounter in her travels: an angel and a Pop diving woman, complete with Ben Day dots and a polka-dotted bikini. Wedged between the travel magazine clichés of the Eiffel Tower and a pyramid are a filigreed crown and a flowered pattern on gold: elegant, aristocratic symbols of femininity. Mrs. Albright's sex will mean different things in the different countries she visits, and the brooch obligingly assembles these meanings for her information.

Robin Kranitzky and Kim Overstreet are as concerned with what Secretary Albright thinks of herself as what the world does. In *Profile of a Woman, Sept./97*, they provide a view inside the beehive hair of a Federalist woman with laurels on her brow and a red-white-and-blue ruffle on her neckline. Written on her hair are snippets of a magazine profile on the Secretary: "A life spent leaving nothing to chance...high standards for excellence, integrity and discipline...Appointed by Clinton...First woman Secretary of State...grew up in four countries...speaks five languages...highest ranking Cabinet member...complicated identity." The quotations continue, with "Float like a butterfly, sting like a bee" appearing twice. But beneath the beehive of hair, Overstreet and Kranitzky present the contents of this "complex identity." Mrs. Albright's brain relates the whole world to the U.S. Capitol, and includes stars, birds, and men.

Bussi Buhs's brooches present perhaps the biggest challenge to Mrs. Albright's sense of humor. *Shoulder Piece* is an epaulette made out of flesh-colored plastic breasts with chrome yellow aureolas and orange nipples. This shoulder plate is thus a transposed "breast plate," with naked breasts forming the shoulder pad of power dressing. A powerful woman may use her femininity as armor, her breasts becoming bristling studs that strengthen her. As a political warrior, her femininity is part of her arsenal of weapons. She wears it, deploys it. The piece is a pretty, if plastic, stylization--colorful, intricate, well contoured. It suggests, too, that there is something inescapably funny about a female warrior, and especially one who has such a chip on her shoulder.

More grotesque is Buhs's *Ceremonial Beard.* It is a latex beard reminiscent of Uncle Sam's white goatee, which is worn by attaching its gauze ribbons to a cheap metal headband. The beard has a strange genesis. Buhs chopped down a giant hogweed in her garden to stop it from spreading its seeds. When she examined the plant, she could not find its hypocotyl: the point where the root begins and the stem ends, where the plant pushes its stem up and its root down. She poured rubber into the hollow stem to document this quandary, and decided that "the parallels to politics are easy to find."[ix] America is the giant hogweed whose seeds she wants to contain and the rationale for whose judgments of "thumbs up, thumbs down" are as hard to locate as the hogweed's hypocotyl. The inside of the hollow giant becomes a grotesque beard for its female wearer. By impersonating Uncle Sam in this gender-bending performance piece, Secretary Albright would surely impede the spreading of the giant's influence.

The "investigation" of the Secretary of State carried out in this exhibition could not have produced the same revelations in any other medium. For brooches, at least in the United States, are a largely feminine symbol system, worn on female clothing and scaled to the female body. They make meaning out of materials that themselves signify value – the preciousness of gold and gemstones, the social values of prestige, beauty, and taste. Mrs. Albright, recognizing in brooches the confluence of issues that define her position in the world, has used them to promote her aims. This exhibition expands her insight through the creativity of these diverse international artists.

WENDY STEINER

Chair, English Department
University of Pennsylvania
July, 1998

ⁱ Alain L. Sanders, "Brooching the Subject Diplomatically," *Time* 3/24/1997: 36.

ⁱⁱ Steven Erlanger, "A Diplomat Who Says 'Read My Pins,'" *New York Times*, "Week in Review," 5/24/1998: 2.

ⁱⁱⁱ Letter to Helen Drutt, 1/19/98.

^{iv} Letter to Helen Drutt, 1/19/98.

^v Letter to Helen Drutt, 12/11/97.

^{vi} Peter Dormer's text, in Helen Drutt English and Peter Dormer, *Jewelry of Our Time: Art, Ornament and Obsession* (New York: Rizzoli International, 1995), p. 184.

^{vii} Susanne Gaensheimer, "Anti-monumentality: Strategies of Democratization in Contemporary German Art," *Index. Contemporary Art and Culture*, 3.-4.97:40-44/91-93.

^{viii} Peter Dormer and Ralph Turner, *The New Jewelry: Trends and Traditions*, revised edition (London: Thames & Hudson, 1994), p. 184.

^{ix} Letter to Helen Drutt, 10/27/97.

Catalogue of the Works

Robert Baines
Australia

Oz is a colloquialism for Australia and
the 'Oz Brooch' comments on the
ambiguity of the land and the politic.

The geographic centre which is
sometime termed 'the outback' is desert
and sometimes called the 'dead heart'.
Others call Canberra, which is the place
of national government, the 'dead
heart'. It seems so often that political
decisions are to the detriment of the
human condition.

Hence, kangaroos looking into the
void.

The Oz Brooch, 1997

STERLING SILVER, POWDER COAT
3" X 3/4"
7,5 X 2 CM

Gijs Bakker

Netherlands

"Liberty" is two real watches in an open
structure. One watch is set upside down
for Mrs. Albright to know how long her
appointment will last and the other for
her visitor to know when to leave.
Of course people may philosophize
about peace, time, distance, diplomacy
etc., etc. but I think that politics are
very one-dimensional.

Liberty, 1997

SILVER, WATCHES
4" X 4 1/2"
9,5 X 11,5 CM

Joan Fraerman Binkley

United States of America

Untitled, 1998

BEADS, FOUND OBJECT
5 1/4" X 2 1/4" X 1/2"
13,5 X 5,5 X 1,3 CM

Manfred Bischoff

Italy

Workingman Hero, 1989

SILVER, GOLD, CORAL
3 3/4" X 3"
9,5 X 7,6 CM

Bussi Buhs

Germany

In my garden grew a giant hogweed.
(Heracleum mantegazzianum)
I cut it off to prevent the seeds from
spreading. The now visible hollow of
the stalk made me very curious. I asked
myself if it could be possible to find
the point from which the plant decides
to push the root downwards and the
stem upwards. (Its Latin name is
hypocotyl).

So I poured fluid silicone rubber in
the hollow, then cautiously dug it all
out and removed the remains of the
plant.

I often practice these kinds of natural
studies.

The result was very fascinating for
me, but I couldn't find the point where
the root begins and the stem ends. A
professor for biology from Munich
University told me that the hypocotyl
is not marked decidedly, it is an area.

Shoulder Piece, 1997

POLYESTER
2 1/4" X 5 7/8" X 4 3/8"
5,7 X 12,3 X 11 CM

I think the parallels to politics are
easily to find: America as a giant...
(In German the words have more and
various colors! RIESENB+RENKLAU –
Giant bear claw, HERKULESSTAUDE –
Hercules shrub, RIESENKERBEL –
Giant chervil) all its numerous "seeds",
and the archetypal ways of decision:
thumb up, thumb down...

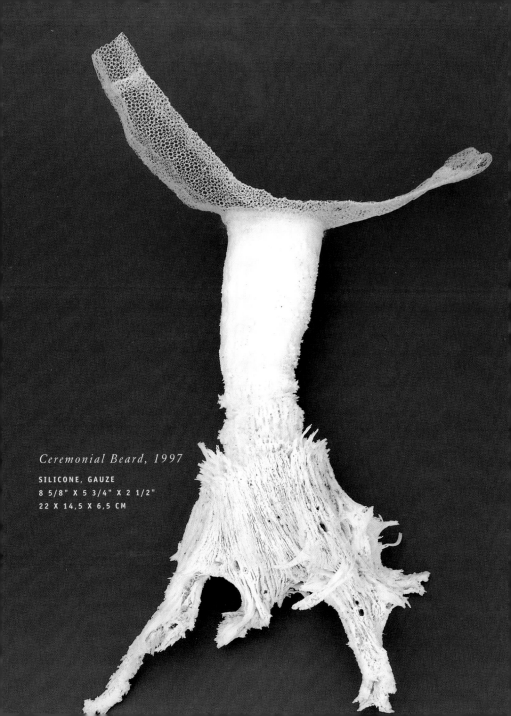

Ceremonial Beard, 1997

SILICONE, GAUZE
8 5/8" X 5 3/4" X 2 1/2"
22 X 14,5 X 6,5 CM

Pierre Cavalan
Australia

I use bits of costume jewelry, semi-precious stones, and Australian trinkets – objects that will help to tell a story or make a statement

The centerpiece from this Grand Order of the Australian American Friendship is a pin from the Australian American Association that shows a kangaroo shaking "hands" with an eagle; it is surrounded by the dual white swans insignia of Canberra. "Pipi" (clam shells) – a symbol of Aboriginal culture is also part of the assemblage.

Simulacre, 1997
ASSEMBLED FOUND AND ANTIQUE OBJECTS
5 1/2" X 3 1/4"
14 X 8 CM

Her Master's Voice, 1997

ASSEMBLED FOUND AND
ANTIQUE OBJECTS
5 1/2" X 4"
13,5 X 10 CM

Kai Chan
Canada

Mountains & Seas, 1997

BALSA WOOD, WATERCOLOR, POLYURETHEAN
2 3/4" X 4 3/4" X 5/8"
7 X 12 X 1,7 CM

Peter Chang

Scotland

Untitled, 1997

POLYESTER RESIN, SILVER
4 3/4" X 2 3/4" X 1"
12 X 7 X 2,5 CM

Sharon Church
United States of America

"Speak softly and carry a big stick..." This was the jingo that defined American foreign diplomacy just a century ago as we were first learning to flex our political muscle. Our nascent military bravado now seems crude when compared to the subtle persuasion of late twentieth century American wealth and influence.

"Speak Softly..." represents the soybean plant ready for harvest. Each year America produces the second largest soy crop in the world. Our land is still a veritable breadbasket, producing this protein rich food that feeds many developing countries and may very well feed us all in the future. As the need for foreign resources has historically linked the world in negotiation and trade, this magnificent bean represents a means to arbitration and resolution, to health and opportunity. We have a big stick.

The second and related piece, "Scatter Pins", begs the question of responsibility and obligation, generosity and return. What does it mean to be the most powerful country in the world: Will we reap what we sow?

Scatter the seed. Speak softly.

Scatter Pins, 1998

CARVED LEMON WOOD, 14 K GOLD, BUFFALO
HORN AND WHITE SAPPHIRES (5 ELEMENTS)
7" X 1 1/3" X 1"
17,8 X 3,5 X 2,5 CM

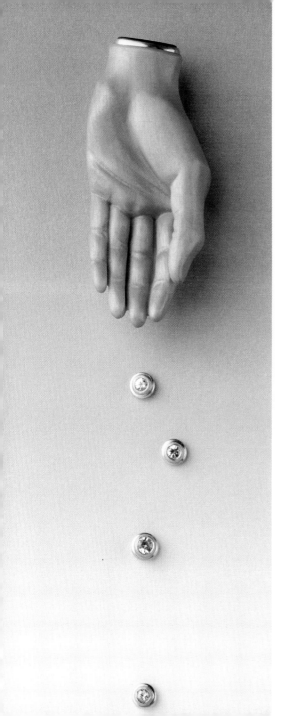

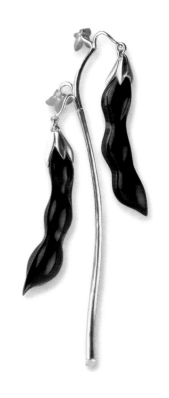

Speak Softly, 1998

**14 K YELLOW GOLD,
CARVED BUFFALO HORN**
8" X 1 1/2" X 1"
20,3 X 4 X 2,5 CM

Hilde De Decker

Belgium

E Pluribus Unum, 1998

18 K GOLD 725 SILVER, COPPER
4 3/4" X 3 7/8"
12 X 10 CM

Georg Dobler

Germany

Both brooches play with the formal richness of nature, utilize the unsurpassed aesthetic of flowers. The ephemeral beauty of the living is preserved in its ideal state. The fruit – that which is sweet and nourishing – is represented by the crystals. An artificial arrangement.

The dark, colorless silver fades away; the form vanishes. Silver: the symbol of the moon, of the night. Soft violet: the color of the spiritual. Reflection instead of action.

The bright, magnificent gold stands out; the form becomes powerful. Gold: the symbol of the sun, of power. The spiritual symbolized in the violet. Thought and action.

Untitled, 1997

SILVER, AMETHYST
2 3/4" X 1 7/8" X 1 1/4"
7 X 4,7 X 3,1 CM

Untitled, 1997

18 K GOLD, AMETHYST
2 3/4" X 1 1/2" X 1 1/8"
7 X 3,8 X 2,8 CM

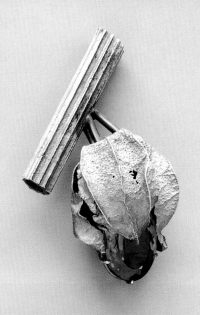

Sandra Enterline

United States of America

Queen Bee, 1998

18 K GOLD, HYMENOPTERA, CROCUS
SATIVUS (POLLEN), GLASS
1 1/2" X 1/2"
3,8 X 1,2 CM

Arline M. Fisch

United States of America

"Ruffled Banner" was inspired by actual flags which wave and flutter in the breeze, constant in their integrity but responsive to the winds of change. The barely seen knot inlaid into the surface is intended to appear and disappear as the light changes, a reference to the sometimes difficult negotiations undertaken in the national interest.

"A Closer Look" is a star-studded banner surrounding a bifocal magnifying glass. From a distance the glass provides either a reflective or a clear view depending upon the perspective of the viewer. If necessary the glass enables the close, and closer, examination of details. This is a private function known only to the wearer.

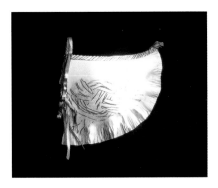

Ruffled Banner, 1997

STERLING SILVER, COPPER, BRASS INLAY
2 3/4" X 2 3/4"
7 X 7 CM

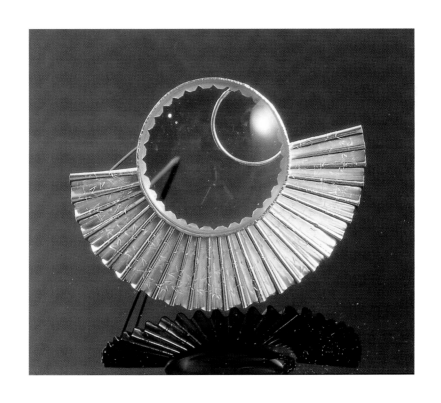

A Closer Look, 1997

STERLING SILVER, 18K GOLD, PLASTIC LENS
2 1/2" X 3 1/4"
6,4 X 8,3 CM

Karl Fritsch

Germany

It is a multicultural brooch; she can go
anywhere with it. It's subtle and strong
at the same time.

Untitled, 1997

OXIDIZED COPPER, GOLD, STEEL
1" X 1/2"
2,5 X 1,2 CM

2 Pieces, Untitled, 1997

GOLD
2" X 2"
5 X 5 CM

2 1/2" X 2 1/2"
6,3 X 6,3 CM

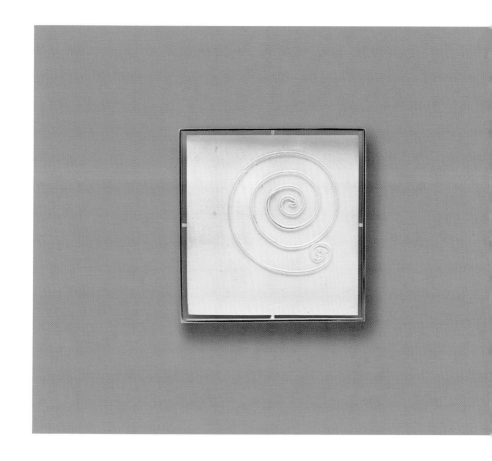

Thomas Gentille

United States of America

PURITY or metal its form and surface
truly sung

CLEAN and clear as the sound of
freedom truly rung

Untitled, 1997

ALUMINIUM
2 3/8" X 2 3/8" X 1/2"
6 X 6 X 0,3 CM

Laurie J. Hall

United States of America

GIVE ME THE LIBERTY TO KNOW,
TO UTTER, AND TO ARGUE FREELY
ACCORDING TO CONSCIENCE,
ABOVE ALL LIBERTIES.

John Milton 1608-1674

Scissors are an artist's tool. Cutting is an inch by inch piece by piece process used to create. I often employ my grandmother's haircutting shears to cut the metal pieces that are taking form before me. I construct and build as I go along.

I like to play with multiple meanings. Real things such as a pair of scissors are a tool but can take on a visual role in the form of an ideogram and convey larger implications.

"Cutting" through conscience is having a sensitive regard for fairness and justice. This quality is central to Ms. Albright's role as Secretary of State. In bringing her social and political conscience to bear, Madeleine Albright cuts new forms and enhances a vision of our nation

Cutting, 1998

STERLING SILVER, 24 K GOLD
2" X 6" X 3/8"
5,1 X 15,2 X 1 CM

William Harper

United States of America

Shiva's Golden Shaft,
Rajasthan Series, 1989

GOLD, ENAMEL
5 3/4" X 1 1/2"
14,7 X 4 CM

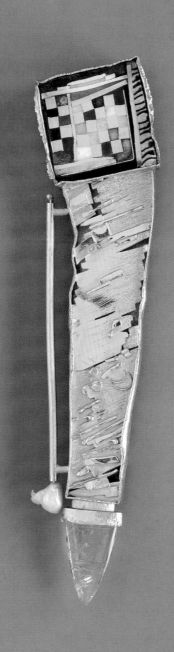

Juhani Heikkilä

Finland

Homo communicans, 1997

BRONZE, VARIOUS WOODS
4" X 3 1/2"
10 X 9 CM

Yasuki Hiramatsu

Japan

The work represents the harmony of the
five continents on earth, and the wish
for world conservation and peace.

Untitled, 1998

24 K GOLD SHEET
2 2/8" X 1 3/8" X 5/8"
5,6 X 3,7 X 1,8 CM

Ron Ho

United States of America

For the Chinese, the dragon is the symbol of power and wisdom, both qualities inherent in Madeleine Albright as she troubleshoots world situations.

The Inspector General, 1998

BRONZE, GOLD, PLATED SILVER, SILVER, EYE GLASS LENS
2" X 1 3/4" X 1/4"
5,1 X 4,5 X 0,7 CM

Daniel Jocz

United States of America

To me diplomacy sometimes becomes a
form of verbal punching. Though the
piece may seem to be a contradiction to
diplomacy, it is how I see Madeleine
Albright, as a person able to deliver the
ultimate punch in negotiations.

Punch (A Change of Mind), 1997

18 K YELLOW GOLD

1 5/8" X 2 1/8" X 1 1/4"

4,2 X 5,3 X 3,2 CM

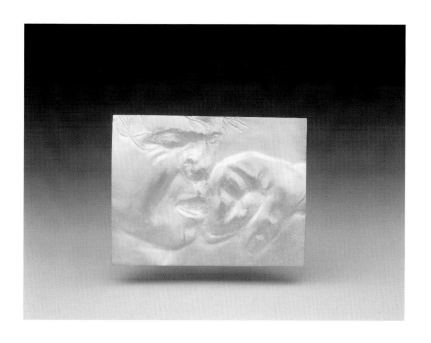

Beppe Kessler

Netherlands

There is more than what you see.

   You cannot read the entire text in the brooch – parts are hidden. I leave it to the imagination of the one wearing the brooch and also the one beholding the brooch. It may entice people as well as inspire conversation.

Inspired, 1998

PLEXI, FABRIC, PAINT, NEWSPRINT
1 1/2" X 1 1/2" X 3/4"
4 X 4 X 2 CM

It Is, 1998

PLEXI, FABRIC, PAINT, NEWSPRINT
1 3/4" X 1 1/2" X 5/8"
4,5 X 4 X 1,5 CM

United States of America

"World Peace" is like a badge of honor.
Ms. Liberty at the top and the peace
dove at the bottom. The center portion
represents Madeleine Albright traveling
the world map for world peace.

   "Earth Angel" represents a strong and
worldly force over seeing world powers.
Wings like a hawk or angel cover the
countries. A woman courageously
diving into the foreign-policy
establishment pool.

World Peace, 1998

STERLING SILVER, BRONZE,
COPPER, NICKEL, PAPER
1 1/2" X 3"
3,8 X 7,6 CM

Earth Angel, 1994

FOIL, PLASTIC, PAPER,
BRONZE, FOUND OBJECT
3" X 4"
7,6 X 10,2 CM

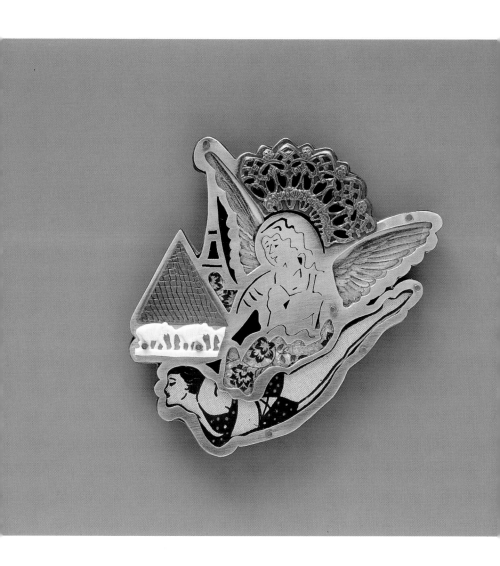

Esther Knobel

Israel

Kisses from Jerusalem, 1998

SILVER, PLASTIC, PAPER, FOUND OBJECT
5/8" X 5/8" X 3/8" OVERALL 1 1/2"
1,6 X 2,2, X 1,2 CM OVERALL 4 CM

"A life spent leaving nothing to
chance...high standards for excellence,
integrity and discipline...Appointed by
Clinton...First woman Secretary of
State...grew up in four countries...speaks
five languages...highest ranking Cabinet
member...complicated identity...first
Cabinet member in order of succession
to the President...floats like a butterfly
stings like a bee...principle advisor to
the President in determining and
carrying out U.S. and foreign
policy...floats like a butterfly and
stings like a bee."

Profile of a Woman, 1997

MICARTA, POLYMER CLAY, COPPER AND GOLD LEAF,
BALSA, GLASS BEAD, COPPER, BRASS, SILVER,
BEE WINGS AND POSTCARD FRAGMENTS
4 3/4" X 3" X 3/4"
12 X 7,6 X 2 CM

Catherine Martin

England

Thinking about the role of a Secretary of State took me into the realms of diplomacy, negotiation, compromise and a willingness to find a middle way between opposing views and this is what the brooch is about........

The base of the brooch is rigid but the two ends bend towards each other yet do not meet but coil in opposite directions: one to the east and one to the west. Both can be moved but cannot physically join............

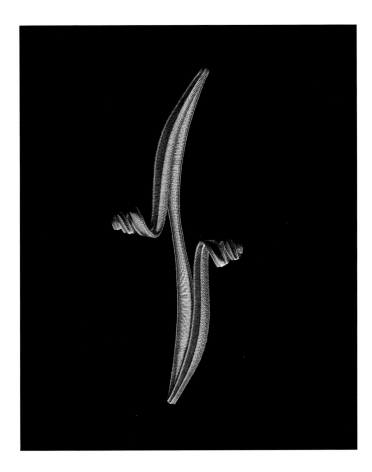

Untitled, 1998

18 K GOLD
3 1/2" X 1 1/2"
9 X 3,8 CM

Richard W. Mawdsley

United States of America

Untitled, 1998

18 K YELLOW GOLD AND WHITE GOLD, PEARLS
PATTERN WELDED STEEL BY DARYL MEIER
3 3/4" X 2 3/4"
9,5 X 7 CM

Bruce Metcalf

United States of America

Figure pin # 145, 1997

MAPLE, BRASS, 14 K GOLD, CHERRY, 23 K
GOLD LEAF
5" X 2 3/4" X 1/2"
12,7 X 7 X 1,3 CM

Louis Mueller

United States of America

I appropriated the lay out "subscribe"
from a subscription form I found in the
magazine ARTFORUM, perhaps
America's most abstract periodical of
ART.

As an American I thought it
appropriate to send a representative of
State wearing a badge of culture in a less
than apparent form, this is a cultural
badge for insiders.

It is my personal statement in assisting
Madeleine Albright in her efforts to
perpetuate internationally a vigorous
interest in the visual arts.

ARTFORUM, 1998

STERLING SILVER, EPOXY
3" X 3" X 1/2"
7,6 X 7,6 X 1,3 CM

Breon O'Casey

England

The story goes that in the Greece of
300 BC, a group of young Greeks were
arguing about what was art and what
wasn't and why and how. And they
decided to go and ask Praxiteles, the
most famous of all the sculptors. So
they went to his workshop and they
asked: "Praxiteles, what is the secret of
your art?" And he answered in four
simple words. He answered: "Oh, I
chip away."

Untitled, c.1990

SILVER, GOLD
1 3/4" X 2 1/4"
4,5 X 5,5 CM

Judy Onofrio
United States of America

Untitled, 1997

ANTIQUE COST JEWELRY, FOUND OBJECTS, BEADS
5 1/2" X 4" X 2 1/2"
14 X 10 X 6,5 CM

Pavel Opočenský

Czech Republic

Untitled, 1997

CZECH NEFRITE
2" X 3" X 1/4"
5,1 X 7,6 X 0,5 CM

Ruudt Peters
Netherlands

The cast shape refers to crystalline
structures which might have originated
in some kind of electrolytic bath. The
spiral wires suggest that electricity
played a role in the process of
crystallization...With the magic of
alchemy he seeks the designer's gold,
which once might have just been called
Beauty. It is a reaction against modern
alchemists who manipulate life with the
steer of sixty who is made pregnant,
and all the genetically altered potatoes,
pigs, tomatoes and peppers.

Reyer Kras
Curator, Stedelijk Museum, Amsterdam

David, 1997

SILVER/JADE IN SANDROSE
4 1/2" X 2" X 1 1/2"
11 X 5 X 4 CM

Wendy Ramshaw

England

I think this is an appropriate piece for
somebody who must depend upon logic
and flashes of perception. "Lightning"
could also act as a conductor and
conduit for rational lateral thinking. It
is the expression of a moment of
energy.

Lightning c. 1989

SILVER WITH 18 K YELLOW GOLD,
AMETHYSTS, MOONSTONE
5 1/8" X 2 1/8"
13 X 5,5 CM

Debra Rapoport

United States of America

Grace, 1998

PAINTED WAXED PAPER, CLOTH, STONES, CRYSTAL, TINSEL, METAL,
PAPER, WAXED LINEN, WIRE (FELT BACKING)
4 1/2" X 9" X 1 1/2"
11,5 X 23 X 4 CM

Gerd Rothmann

Germany

The brooch is conceived as a gift from
the Secretary of State as a momento of
her official visits, both foreign and
domestic.

The fingerprint is both signature and
signet. Its fine lines have the effect of a
drawing or an ornament. The brooch,
is a personal gesture and a sign of
solidarity from Mrs. Albright.

WITH HONOR AND GRATITUDE

PRESENTED BY

THE SECRETARY OF STATE

MADELEINE K. ALBRIGHT

Honor/Gratitude Multiple, 1998 Model for Brooch

GOLD, SILVER, HANDMADE PAPER BOX
1 1/4" X 3"
3,2 X 7,6 CM

Margareth Sandström
Sweden

Peace Angel, 1997

GOLD, DIAMONDS
3 1/2" X 3"
9 X 7,6 CM

Lucy Sarneel

Netherlands

"This brooch is a metaphor for seeing
and hearing the world events with a
wise view and insight

See-Ear, 1997

ZINC, PAINT
2 1/2" X 2" X 1 3/4"
6,4 X 5 X 4,5 CM

Marjorie Schick

United States of America

My work is an exploration of three-dimensional forms which relate both to the human body and to the environment as free-standing sculptures. They are created in a variety of materials including metal, wood, papier-mâché, canvas, and paint. Color and surface decoration are of equal importance to the structure as it exists in space and for wearing.

"Liberty Torch" exemplifies my current artistic direction, a dialogue about experiences and places. This piece makes reference to a symbol from American history, an object held by the Statue of Liberty. While the symbol is historical, the style is current, of the 90s.

Liberty Torch, 1997

PAPIER-MACHÉ
6" X 5 1/8" X 1 7/8"
15,2 X 13 X 4,7 CM

Bernard Schobinger
Switzerland

Found Objects, 1979/89
ZINC SHEET, STEEL, COPPER, ZINC
2 3/4" X 3 1/4"
7 X 8,2 CM

Deganit Schocken

Israel

These pieces express tension in
territorial difference. Disjunctive
elements find their home in relation to
one another as they merge in one
geography. Integrity depends on a
response that is prepared to strain for
harmony, beauty and peace. We share
olive trees and sand in the Middle East.
We must reconcile our differences.

Territories, 1995

SILVER, JADE
2" X 4 7/8" X 3/4"
5 X 12,2, X 2 CM

SILVER, CLOTH
2 1/4" X 3 3/4"
5,7 X 9,5 CM

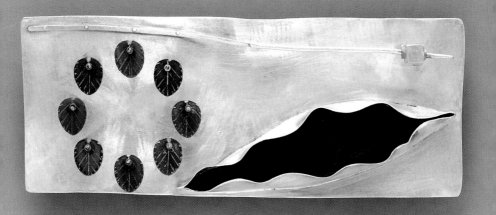

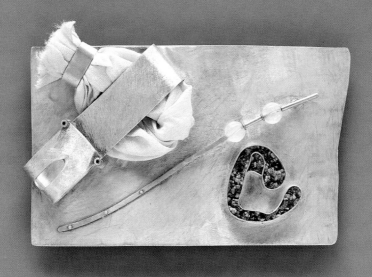

Joyce J. Scott

United States of America

Liberty, 1998

**BEADS; PEYOTE STITCH
6" X 3 1/2"
15,2 X 8,9 CM**

Barbara Seidenath

United States of America

I consider myself a goldsmith using
traditional techniques to create wearable
pieces of personal ornament.

By choosing the adequate form to
materialize an idea and applying my
knowledge of color and materials and
their specific effects, I determine the
expression of that piece. I am also
trying to bring into this work a certain
ambiguity that allows the wearer and the
viewer room for personal interpretation.

Finding the right balance between
mysticism and revelation in the pursuit
of a beautiful object presents a challenge
to me.

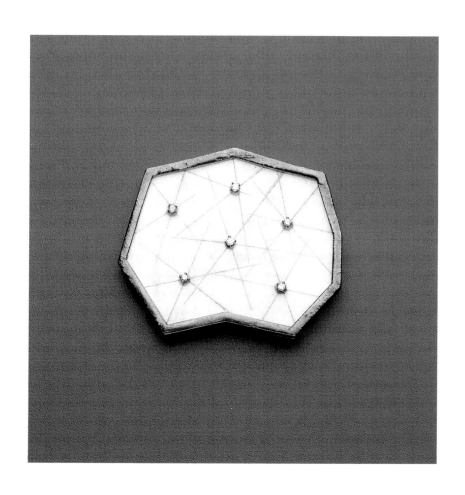

Untitled, 1998

STERLING SILVER, ENAMEL, DIAMONDS,
NIELLO
2" X 2 1/2"
5 X 6,3 CM

Stephan Seyffert

Germany

Article of Value, c. 1993

GOLD
1 1/2" X 3 1/8" X 1"
4 X 7,9 X 2,5 CM

Sondra Sherman

United States of America

This piece reminds us of the preciousness of our world and the fluidity of its
constellation. The globe is a large gem,
the continents gold and free floating.
It looks like a big opal.

Continental Drift, 1998

STERLING SILVER, 22 K GOLD, ACETATE, WATER
2 1/4" X 1" X 1/4"
5,7 X 2,5 X 0,5 CM

Helen Shirk

United States of America

My effort in making this piece was to
embody the organic nature of
negotiation – the essential and delicate
areas of compromise and agreement
within the whole, the continued
strength and resiliency necessary to
accomplish this task. These aspects also
reflect the way in which Madeleine
Albright has successfully negotiated the
path of her own life to become
America's first woman Secretary of
State.

Untitled, 1998

SILVER, GOLD
4 1/8" X 1 1/2" X 3/4"
10,5 X 4 X 2 CM

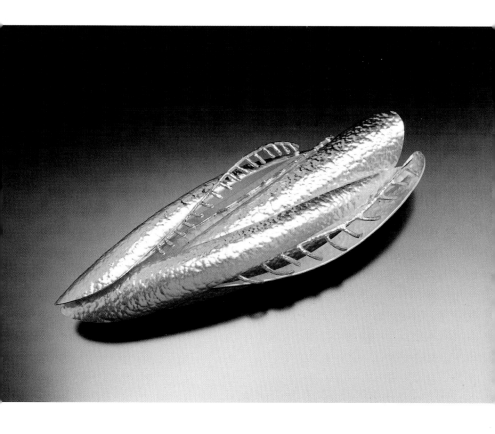

Jiří Šibor
Czech Republic

Sitting in the cabin of a plane, I saw a flight video with the images of directions between continents and the TV news. The news included a clip about the visit of the Secretary of State. Later, I opened The New York Times and read the "Weather Report," on the side where there were small maps of the U.S.A.

An idea was born– a map of the U.S.A. as symbol of the landscape of a large country seen from above.

I used reconstructed coral for the surface area of the U.S.A. with borders for individual states. The red color of the matter is cordial and bright like the personage and name - Madeleine K. Albright; the base is stainless steel, a rust-resistant symbol for the future.

(Today, July 14th, 1997, the Secretary of State of the United States is presently in Prague, visiting the Czech Republic – this is the best reason for the sending of the work – as the last point of the idea!)

The United States, 1997

RECONSTRUCTED CORAL,
STAINLESS STEEL
2" X 1 3/4" X 1/4" (USA);
1" X 1" X 1/4" (ALASKA)
5 X 4,5 X 1,9 CM (USA);
2,5 X 2,2 X 0,7 CM (ALASKA)

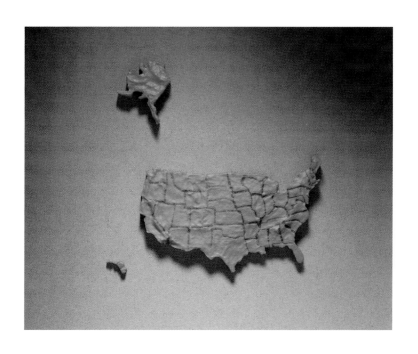

Peter Skubic

Austria

What is important to me as a designer
(jewelry) is the questioning of received
ideas and the examination of the
(design) possibilities of our time.
I work a great deal with high-grade
steel, a material of our century for
which I've developed a technique which
permits me to assemble my creations
with pins rather than soldering or
welding. Naturally, I also work with
gold, albeit differently. I love the
absurd and have thus also invented
invisible jewelry – invisible because the
jewelry doesn't exist.

Untitled, 1997

GOLD
2 1/8" X 1"
5,5 X 2,5 CM

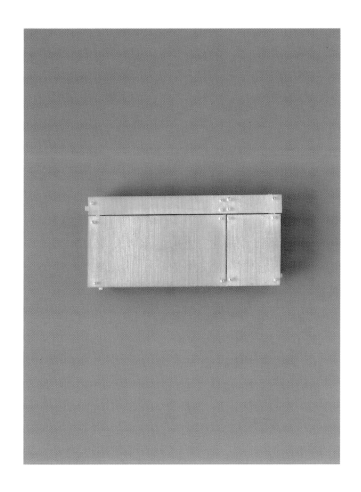

Kiff Slemmons

United States of America

Madeleine Albright wears jewelry as
intellectual armor and as symbolic
language. In a particular way, it is her
voice. That was the spark for me to pay
tribute to her as she has paid tribute to
jewelry.

Liberty Lorgnette, 1997

MIXED METALS
4" X 2 1/2"
10 X 6,3 CM

Mightier Than, 1997

MIXED METALS
2 1/2" X 2 3/4" X 1/4"
6,3 X 7 X 0,7 CM

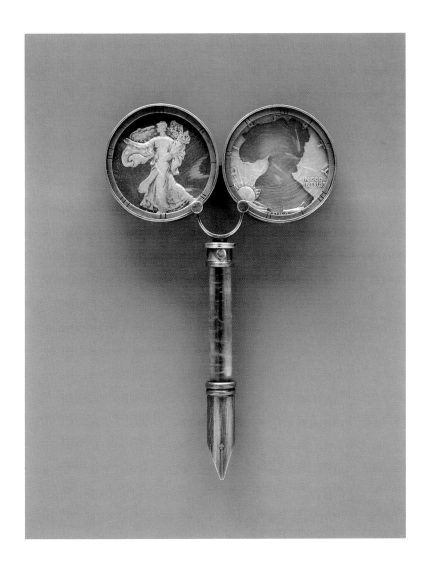

Robert Smit

Netherlands

I gave the proposed topic-Freedom of Choice-considerable thought. An ethical or moral approach seemed self-evident since I live in a country where this theme might well have been invented. The vision and commitment in this design, and its execution, are bound up to my personal history as well as to my conceptions of, and about, freedom (Towards the Liberation of Drawings, 1978, Robert Smit).

Consequently I perceive "Freedom of Choice" as an attitude and stance towards the abuse of power and intolerance, for instance, and towards all kinds of small-minded prohibitions or restrictions laid-down and defined by church and state. This attitude is instinctive. It is directed against every secret, every arrogant representation of things and ideas, against all inflexibility.

While sketching designs there arose a form, almost accidentally, in which plates of molded and decorated gold described a five-sided figure. In the execution it became the occasion for an interpretation of the Pentagon. This "Pentagon-Windmill" brooch is intended as a qualified conception of both the building and the organization. But also it should be seen as a metaphor for that building, that impenetrable fortress.

Pentagon-Windmill, 1997

GOLD 750/000-900/000-1000/000
5 1/2" X 4 4/5" X 1/2"
12,7 X 12,3 X 1,2 CM

Ramona Solberg

United States of America

My pin reflects the way I perceive a
Secretary of State – formal, classic and
a very important person.

Untitled, 1998

BRONZE, SILVER, FOUND OBJECT
4 1/4" X 3 1/2" X 1/2"
2,5 X 7 X 1 CM

Bettina Speckner

Germany

I have chosen these two brooches, because I like the story of their pictures in this context.

The photos I used for my etching are from my mother's album. In 1952, when she was 16, she went with the American Field Service to the USA for one year. She took the photos while entering N.Y. city's harbor (because, of course she went by ship at that time) and during her first walk through Manhattan. For me they show images of the strange and mysterious new continent's city jungle. On the other hand, they also give a calm and quiet, somehow romantic view.

I etched the photos in zinc, because I like this very special cold grey combined with "warm" silver and gold.

Ship with Leave, 1994

**PHOTO ETCHING IN ZINC, SILVER, FOUND
PIECE IN GOLD
1" X 2 3/4" X 1/3"
2,5 X 7 X 1 CM**

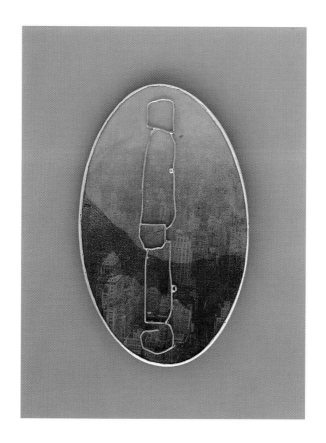

New York, 1997

PHOTO ETCHING IN ZINC, SILVER, GOLD
3" X 2"
7,6 X 5 CM

Tore Svensson

Sweden

When the Paracas Indians in Peru
buried their relatives, they wrapped
them into wonderful decorated weaves
filled with symbols. Some of these
textiles are exhibited in the Ethnographical Museum in Gothenburg,
Sweden. One of the weaves consists of
multiple squares interlocked with each
other with three more squares within.
The idea with my brooches is that
Madeleine Albright, in a symbolic way,
could bring the textiles, with their
symbols, back to where they belong,
when she visits Peru.

Set of Four Brooches, 1998

**IRON, GOLD, SILVER
2 1/4" X 2 1/4"
5,7 X 5,7 CM**

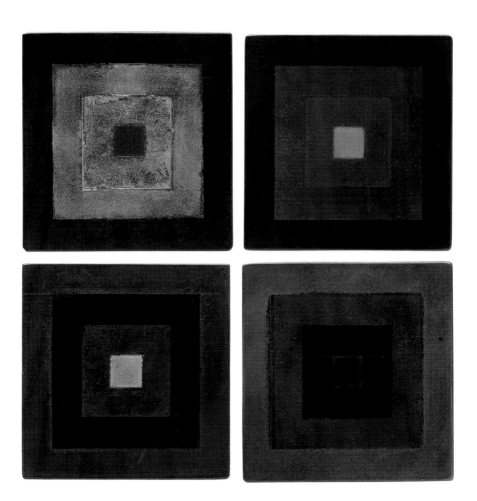

Detlef Thomas
Germany

Untitled, 1997

18 K GOLD, MALACHITE
2 1/2" X 2 1/4 "
6,3 X 5,6 CM

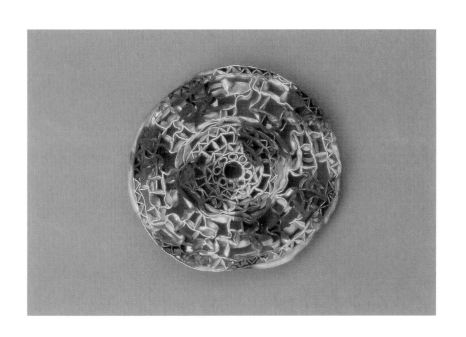

Merrily Tompkins

United States of America

This is a brooch for Madame Albright
to wear when she visits people who
condone the practice of female genital
mutilation. I hope the crude execution
of the piece evokes the vulgar brutality
of those "surgeries". I just have a hard
time believing that the almighty wants
little girls held down and hurt and
robbed like that. These folks need to
take a look in the mirror and say
howdy-doo to Old Bendy himself.

Untitled, 1998

SILVER, SEMI PRECIOUS STONES
2 3/4" X 1 3/4"
7 X 4,5 CM

Karel Votipka

Czech Republic

Untitled, 1998

STEEL, 14 K GOLD, ZIRKOUS, OPAL, BLACK CORAL
4 1/2" X 3" X 1 1/2"
11,5 X 7,6 X 4 CM

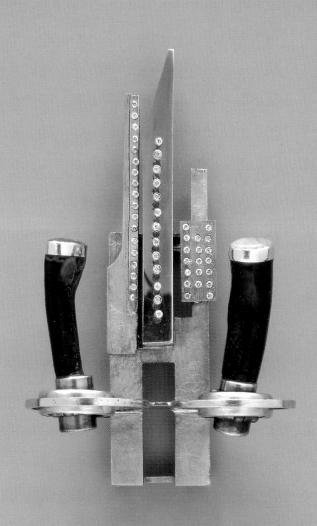

Margaret West

Australia

When we close our eyes against the light we see
red (roses are red)
White clouds veil our eyes from the light
(this rose is white)
Beyond all clouds awaits a sky of blue roses

Cloud Rose, 1997

THASSOS MARBLE, SILVER (925)
2 1/2" X 2 1/2"
6,3 X 6,3 CM

Peter de Wit

Sweden

Washington Monument, 1997

CRYSTAL, DIAMONDS, RUBIES, SAPPHIRES, 18 K GOLD
3 1/2" X 1/2" X 1/2"
9 X 1,3 X 1,3 CM

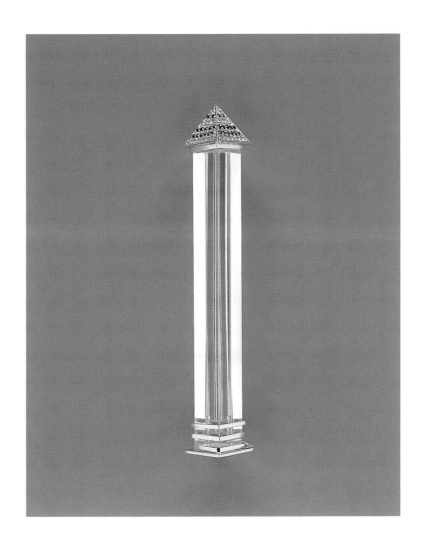

Nancy Worden

United States of America

A handshake is not only a gesture of
courtesy and good will, but can also be
as binding as a contract. I wanted to
design something for Ms. Albright with
an image easily interpreted by people
who do not speak English that
projected the message of friendship,
peace and keeping promises. I titled it
"Arms Agreement" because in all
situations I think we need to have a
little bit of humor.

Arms Agreement, 1998

18 K GOLD, STERLING SILVER
1 3/4" X 2 3/4" X 1/2"
4,5 X 7 X 1,3 CM

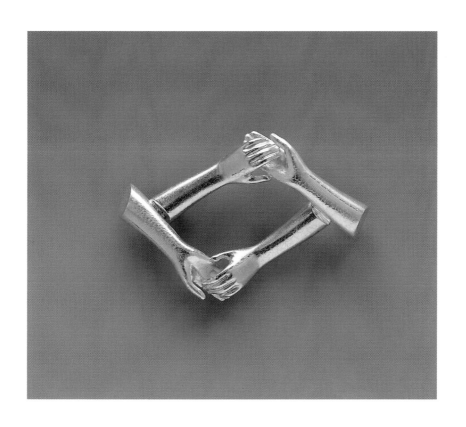

Biographies of the Artists

ROBERT BAINES

BORN:
April 1, 1949, Melbourne, Victoria, Australia

CURRENT RESIDENCE:
Melbourne, Victoria, Australia

SELECTED EXHIBITIONS:
1998 *Jewellery Moves*, National Museums of Scotland, Edinburgh; *Contemporary Jewellery: Value Added*, National Gallery of Victoria, Melbourne; *Schmuck '98*, Internationale Handwerksmesse, Munich; 1997 *Cicely and Colin Rigg Craft Award*, National Gallery of Victoria, Melbourne; *Contemporary Vessels and Jewels*, Shanghai Museum, China; 1996 *Collecting Today for Tomorrow*, Powerhouse Museum, Sydney; *Granulation 1996*, Pforzheim (traveled); 1995 *VicHealth National Craft Award*, National Gallery of Victoria, Melbourne; 1992 *Design Visions: The Second Australian International Crafts Triennial*, Art Gallery of Western Australia

SELECTED PUBLIC COLLECTIONS:
Victoria and Albert Museum, London; Australian National Gallery, Canberra; National Gallery of Victoria, Melbourne; Royal Melbourne Institute of Technology, Victoria; Prime Minister's Department, Canberra; The Victorian State Craft Collection, Meat Market Craft Centre, Melbourne; Waikato Museum of Art and History, Hamilton, New Zealand; Art Gallery of Western Australia, Perth; Art Gallery of South Australia, Adelaide; Powerhouse Museum, Sydney; Waikato Polytechnic, Hamilton, New Zealand; Queensland Art Gallery, Brisbane, Australia

GIJS BAKKER*

BORN:
February 20, 1942, Amersfoort, Netherlands

CURRENT RESIDENCE:
Amsterdam, Netherlands

SELECTED EXHIBITIONS:
1998 *Jewellery Moves*, National Museums of Scotland, Edinburgh; *Subjects: Narratives 98*, Taideteollisuusmuseo, Helsinki, Finland; *Holysport/Shot Project*, Helen Drutt: Philadelphia; Galerie Ra, Amsterdam; *Ad Dekkers in zijn tijd*, Stedelijk Museum, Amsterdam; 1995 *Quatre créateurs de bijoux: Gijs Bakker + Babetto + Dahm + Kruger*, Musée des Arts Decoratifs de la Ville de Lausanne, Switzerland; 1994 *Gijs Bakker: Holes Project*, Galerie Spektrum, Munich; Helen Drutt: Philadelphia; SOFA:Chicago; Galerie Ra, Amsterdam; 1993 *Voorzien: Benno Premsela Applied Art Collection*, Stedelijk Museum, Amsterdam; *Tekens & Ketens*, Museum van der Togt, Amstelveen; Gemeentemuseum, Arnhem, Netherlands;

SELECTED PUBLIC COLLECTIONS:
Museum Boymans-van Beuningen, Rotterdam; Centraal Museum, Utrecht; Cooper-Hewitt, National Museum of Design, Smithsonian Institution, New York; Denver Museum of Art, CO; Gemeentelijke van Reekummuseum, Apeldoorn, Netherlands; Montreal Musée des Arts Décoratifs, Quebec; Museum Het Kruithuis, 's-Hertogenbosch, Netherlands; National Museum of Modern Art, Kyoto; Nordenfjeldske Kunstindustrimuseum, Trondheim, Norway; Power House Museum, Sydney; Rijksdienst Beeldende Kunst, Den Haag, Netherlands; Schmuckmuseum, Pforzheim, Germany; Stedelijk Museum, Amsterdam; Taideteollisuusmuseo, Helsinki

JOAN FRAERMAN BINKLEY*

BORN:
December 4, 1927, Highland Park, IL, USA

CURRENT RESIDENCE:
Highland Park, IL, USA

SELECTED EXHIBITIONS:
1997 Jean Albano Gallery, SOFA: Chicago, IL;
1994 *A Moveable Feast**, Amsterdam; *Schmuck
Unserer Zeit**, Zurich; 1993 *Ahead of Fashion: Hats
of the 20th Century*, Philadelphia Museum of Art,
PA; 1992-93 *Korun Kieli**, Gothenburg; Helsinki;
1990 *Solo Exhibition*, Compass Rose Gallery, Chicago, IL

SELECTED PUBLIC COLLECTIONS:
Springfield Art Museum, IL

MANFRED BISCHOFF*

BORN:
November 7, 1947, Schomberg/Calw, Germany

CURRENT RESIDENCE:
San Casciano dei Bagni, Italy

SELECTED EXHIBITIONS:
1998 *Solo Exhibition*, Sofie Lachaert, Antwerpen;
1996 *Solo Exhibition*, Louise Smit, Amsterdam;
1994 *A Moveable Feast**, Amsterdam; *Schmuck
Unserer Zeit**, Zurich; *Solo Exhibition*, Helen Drutt:
Philadelphia, SOFA: Chicago, IL; 1993 *Facet I*,
Kunsthal, Rotterdam; *üb ersetzen*, solo exhibition,
Museum Het Kruithuis, 's-Hertogenbosch, Netherlands; 1992 *Triennale du Bijou*, Musée des Arts
Décoratifs, Paris; 1991 *Beauty is a Story*, Museum
Het Kruithuis, 's-Hertogenbosch, Netherlands;
1990 *Schmuckszene '90*, Internationale Handwerksmesse, Munich

SELECTED PUBLIC COLLECTIONS:
Danner-Stiftung Collection, Munich; Museum
Het Kruithuis, 's-Hertogenbosch, Netherlands;
Power House Museum, Sydney; Schmuckmuseum, Pforzheim, Germany; Stedelijk Museum,
Amsterdam

BUSSI BUHS

BORN:
June 3, 1940, Mannheim, Germany

CURRENT RESIDENCE:
Hohenzell, Germany

SELECTED EXHIBITIONS:
1998 *Jewellery Moves*, National Museums of Scotland, Edinburgh; *Solo Exhibition*, Galerie Ra, Amsterdam; 1997 *Plastik aus Plastik*, Cubus-Kunsthalle, Duisburg (traveling); 1996 *Du Contemporain, Bijoux et Orfevrerie de créateurs*, Les Musées de Cagnes-Sur-Mer, Côte d'Azur, France; *Schmuck '96*, Sonderschua auf der 48, Internationale Handwerksmesse, Munich; 1995 *Im Garten der Lüste*, solo exhibition, Galerie Biró, Munich

SELECTED PUBLIC COLLECTIONS:
Museum Wiesbaden; Ministerium für Kunst und Wissenschaff, Baden-Würtenberg; Bundestagsgebäude, Bonn

PIERRE CAVALAN*

BORN:
February 16, 1954, Paris, France

CURRENT RESIDENCE:
Glebe, NSW, Australia

SELECTED EXHIBITIONS:
1998 *Jewellery Moves*, National Museums of Scotland, Edinburgh; *Undercurrents*, Itami City Craft Museum and Azabu Museum of Arts and Crafts, Tokyo; *New Jewelry from Australia*, Galerie Ra, Amsterdam; 1997 *Revelations*, National Ornamental Metal Museum, Memphis, TN; 1995 Beaver Galleries, Australia, SOFA: Chicago; 1994 *A Moveable Feast**, Amsterdam; *Schmuck Unserer Zeit**, Zurich

SELECTED PUBLIC COLLECTIONS:
Art Gallery of South Australia, Adelaide; Artbank, Sydney; Craft Council of Northern Territory - Alice Springs Collections; Griffith Regional Gallery, NSW; Montreal Musée des Arts Décoratifs, Quebec; National Gallery of Australia, Canberra; Northern Territory Museum of Arts and Sciences, Darwin; Powerhouse Museum, Sydney; Sydney Town Hall Collection; Tasmanian Museum and Art Gallery, Hobart; Wollongong City Gallery, NSW

KAI CHAN

BORN:
July 25, 1940, Chung Kiang, China

CURRENT RESIDENCE:
Ontario, Canada

SELECTED EXHIBITIONS:
1997 *Common Space International Art Exhibition*, Pexinok, Slovakia; 1995 *8th International Triennial of Tapestry*, Lodz, Poland; *34th Annual Toronto Outdoor Art Exhibition*, Toronto; 1994 *Gold from Straw*, Internationales Schmucksymposion, Köln; 1993 *The 7th Montreal Biennial of Tapestry*, Montreal; 1992 *A Treasury of Canadian Craft*, The Canadian Craft Museum, Vancouver, British Columbia; *Of Magic, Power and Memory*, Bellevue Art Museum, WA

SELECTED PUBLIC COLLECTIONS:
The Canadian Museum of Civilization, Hull, Quebec; The Library and Gallery, Cambridge, Ontario; Montreal Musée des Arts Décoratifs, Quebec Nordenfjeldske Kunstindustrimuseum, Trondheim, Norway; The Canada Council Art Bank, Ottawa; The Ontario Crafts Council, Toronto; Art Gallery of Szombathely, Hungary

PETER CHANG*

BORN:
December 1, 1944, London, England

CURRENT RESIDENCE:
Glasgow, Scotland

SELECTED EXHIBITIONS:
1998 *Jewellery Moves*, National Museums of Scotland, Edinburgh; *Objects of Our Time*, American Craft Museum, New York; 1997 *Designed for Delight: Alternative Aspects of 20th Century Decorative Arts*, Montreal Musée des Arts Décoratifs, Quebec (traveled); 1996 *Solo Exhibition,* Galerie Biró, Munich; *Du Contemporain, Bijoux et Orfevrerie de créateurs,* Les Musées de Cagnes-Sur-Mer, Côte d'Azur, France; *Polymeric Chimera*, Musée d'Art Moderne et d'Art Contemporain, Nice; *Objects of Our Time,* Crafts Council, London; 1995 *Or et Medailles*, World Gold Council, Parc des Expositions de Paris; *Modern British Jewellery*, Landesmuseum, Mainz

SELECTED PUBLIC COLLECTIONS:
Aberdeen Museum, Aberdeen; Cooper-Hewitt, National Museum of Design, Smithsonian Institution, New York; Crafts Council Collection, London Danner-Stiftung Collection, Munich; Taideteollisuusmuseo, Helsinki; Kelvingrove Museum, Glasgow; Montreal Musée des Arts Décoratifs, Quebec; Museum für Angewandte Kunst, Köln; National Museums of Scotland, Edinburgh; Philadelphia Museum of Art, PA; Victoria & Albert Museum, London

SHARON CHURCH

BORN:
October 15, 1948; Richland, WA, USA

CURRENT RESIDENCE:
Philadelphia, PA, USA

SELECTED EXHIBITIONS:
1998 Helen Drutt: Philadelphia, SOFA: New York; 1997 *The Environ Mental Bead*, Brookfield Craft Center, CT; 1996 *New Jewelry from the U.S.A.*, The Edinburgh International Festival Exhibition (traveled); *North American Metal Arts* Invitational: *Heritage and Diversity*, Montgomery College, Rockville, MD; 1995 *Double Vision*, Charles A. Wustum Museum of Fine Arts, Racine, WI; 1990 Contemporary American Craft, Philadelphia Museum of Art, PA

SELECTED PUBLIC COLLECTIONS:
Charles A. Wustum Museum of Fine Arts, Racine, WI; Delaware Art Museum, Wilmington, DE

HILDE DE DECKER

BORN:
January 14, 1965, Dendermonde, Belgium

CURRENT RESIDENCE:
Londerzeel, Belgium

SELECTED EXHIBITIONS:
1998 *Internationale Schmuckszene '98* Handwerksmesse, Munich; Belgische Sieraden, Arvada Center of Arts, Colorado; *Blikvangers*, Textielmuseum, Tilburg, Netherlands; 1997 Parures Cultureel Centrum, Strombeek, Belgium (traveled) *Bullet-Proof Forms*, Museum voor Sierkunst en Vormgeving, Ghent; 1996 *Eva's Kissen*, Galerie V&V, Vienna; *Granulation 1996*, Schmuckmuseum, Pforzheim; *Ig Ag,* Provinciaal Museum Sterckshof-Zilvercentrum, Deurne; *Belgische Sieraden*, Schmuckmuseum, Pforzheim (traveled); 1995 *Sieraad, Symbool, Signaal*, Kon. Fabiolazaal, Antwerpen, Belgium; 1993-94 *Internationale Schmuckszene*, Handwerksmesse, Munchen; 1991 *Multiples*, Gallery Sofie Lachaert, Ghent, Belgium; 1995 *Triennale voor Vormgeving*, Museum voor Sierkunsten, Ghent

GEORG DOBLER*

BORN:
April 6, 1952, Bayreuth, Germany

CURRENT RESIDENCE:
Berlin-Wilmersdorf, Germany

SELECTED EXHIBITIONS:
1998 *Solo Exhibition*, Helen Drutt: Philadelphia; 1997 Grassi Messe '97, Grassi Museum, Leipzig, Germany; *Papiermaché und Gipsstuck*, Kunstgewerbemuseum SMPK, Berlin, Germany; 1996 *Solo Exhibition*, Galerie Ra, Amsterdam, Netherlands; *Hommage à Sospel*, Musée d'Art Moderne et d'Art Contemporain, Nice, France; *Subjects '96*, Retretti Art Centre, Finland; *Ornament Heute*, Bunndesverband Kunsthandw., Frankfurt/M., Germany; 199 *New Times, New Thinking: Jewellery in Europe and America*, Crafts Council, London; National Museum and Gallery, Cardiff, Wales; 1995 *Or et Medailles '95*, World Gold Council, Paris, France; Grassi Messe '95, Grassi Museum, Leipzig, Germany; *Die Sammlung der Dannerstiftung*, Bayerischen Kunstgewerbeverein, Munich; Schmuckmuseum Pforzheim, Germany

SELECTED PUBLIC COLLECTIONS:
Art Gallery of Western Australia, Perth; Badisches Landsmuseum, Karlsruhe; Danner-Stiftung Collection, Munich; Det Danske Kunstindustrimuseum, Copenhagen; Honolulu Academy of Art, Honolulu; Grassi Museum, Leipzig; Israel Museum, Jerusalem; Kunstgewerbemuseum, Berlin; Kunstindustrimuseet i Oslo; Museum Ceskeho Rajé, Turnov; Museum für Angewandte Kunst, Vienna; Museum für Kunst und Gewerbe, Hamburg; Museum Het Kruithuis, 's-Hertogenbosch; National Museum of Modern Art, Kyoto; Njordenfeldske Kunstindustrimuseum, Trondheim, Norway; Schmuckmuseum, Pforzheim, Germany; Stadtmuseum München, Munich; Stedelijk Museum, Amsterdam; Taideteollisuusmuseo, Helsinki

SANDRA ENTERLINE

BORN:
April 20, 1960, Oil City, PA, USA

CURRENT RESIDENCE:
San Francisco, CA, USA

SELECTED EXHIBITIONS:
1998 *Jewellery Moves*, National Museums of Scotland, Edinburgh; 1997 *Celebrating American Craft, 1975-1995*, Det Danske Kunstindustriemuseum, Copenhagen, Denmark; 1996 *Signals: Late Twentieth- Century American Jewelry*, Cranbrook Art Museum, Bloomfield Hills, MI; Montreal Musée des Arts Décoratifs, Quebec; *New Times, New Thinking: Jewellery in Europe and America*, Crafts Council, London; National Museum and Gallery, Cardiff, Wales; *Breaking Ground*, solo exhibition, Susan Cummins Gallery, Mil Valley, CA; 1995 *Double Vision*, Charles A. Wustum Museum of Fine Arts, Racine, WI; *Chicago International New Art Forms*, 1988-1997, Susan Cummins Gallery, Mill Valley, CA

PUBLIC COLLECTIONS:
American Craft Museum, New York; Oakland Museum of Art, Oakland, CA; Charles A. Wustum Museum of Fine Arts, Racine, WI

ARLINE M. FISCH*

BORN:
August 21, 1931, Brooklyn, NY, USA

CURRENT RESIDENCE:
San Diego, CA, USA

SELECTED EXHIBITIONS:
1998 *Jewellery Moves*, National Museums of Scotland, Edinburgh, 1997 *Celebrating American Craft, 1975-1995,* Det Danske Kunstindustrimuseum, Copenhagen; *Portrait of Masters in the Crafts*, Internationale Handwerksmesse, Munich; *Designed for Delight: Alternative Aspects of 20th Century Decorative Arts*, Montreal Musée des Arts Décoratifs, Quebec (traveled); 1996 *School of Fisch*, Craft & Folk Art Museum, Los Angeles, CA; *Just Add Water: Artists and the Aqueous World*, Wustum Museum, Racine, WI; *New Times, New Thinking: Jewellery in Europe and America*, Crafts Council, London; 1995 *The New Basket*, Arkansas Arts Center, Little Rock, AK

SELECTED PUBLIC COLLECTIONS:
American Craft Museum, New York; Arkansas Arts Center, Little Rock, AK; Art Gallery of Western Australia, Perth, Australia; Charles A. Wustum Museum of Fine Arts, Racine, WI; Detroit Institute of the Arts, Detroit, MI; Det Danske Kunstindustrimuseum, Copenhagen; Kunstindustrimuseet i Oslo, Norway; Minnesota Museum of Art, St. Paul, MN; Musée des Arts Décoratifs, Montreal; Nordenfjeldske Kunstindustrimuseum, Trondheim, Norway; Museum of Fine Arts, Boston, MA; National Museum of Modern Art, Kyoto, Japan; Oakland Museum, Oakland, CA; Renwick Gallery, NMAA, Smithsonian Institution, Washington, D.C; Royal Scottish Museum, Edinburgh Schmuckmuseum, Pforzheim, Germany; Vatican Museum, Vatican City; Victoria & Albert Museum, London

KARL FRITSCH

BORN:
March 10, 1963, Sonthofen, Germany

CURRENT RESIDENCE:
Munich, Germany

SELECTED EXHIBITIONS:
1998 *Jewellery Moves*, National Museums of Scotland, Edinburgh; 1996 *Vorschläge der Jury, Förderpreise; 1996*, Künstlerwerkstatt Lothringerstrass, Munich; 1995 *Schmuckszene '95*, Internationale Handwerksmesse, Munich; *Vorschläge der Jury, Forderpreise 1995*, Künstlerwerkstatt Lothringerstrass, Munich; *Neuerwerbungen*, Stedelijk Museum, Amsterdam; Gallery Jewelerswerk at the International Craft Fair, Chicago; *Jahresgaben*, Kunstverein München

SELECTED PUBLIC COLLECTIONS:
Stedelijk Museum, Amsterdam, Netherlands; Hiko Mizumo College of Jewellery, Tokyo, Japan; Jewellery and Gemstone Museum, Turnov, Czech Republic; Danner-Stiftung, Munich, Germany; Angermuseum, Erfurt, Germany

MAX FRÖHLICH*

BORN:
December 16, 1908, Ennenda, Kt. Glarus, Switzerland

DIED:
October 24, 1997, Zurich, Switzerland

SELECTED EXHIBITIONS:
1994 *A Moveable Feast**, Amsterdam; *Schmuck Unserer Zeit**, Zurich; *Schmuck und Gerät*, Deutsches Goldschmiedehaus, Hanau, Germany (traveled); 1993 *Contemporary Jewelry**, Little Rock, AK; *Schmuckszene '93*, Internationale Handwerksmesse, Munich; 1992-93 *Korun Kieli**, Gothenburg; Helsinki; 1988-89 *Solo Exhibition*, Helen Drutt: New York; 1983 *Solo Exhibition*, Kunstgewerbemuseum, Museum Für Gestaltung, Zurich

SELECTED PUBLIC COLLECTIONS:
Heimatwerk, Zurich; Kunstgewerbemuseum, Zurich; Schmuckmuseum, Pforzheim, Germany

THOMAS GENTILLE*

BORN:
August 11, 1936, Mansfield, OH, USA

CURRENT RESIDENCE:
New York, NY, USA

SELECTED EXHIBITIONS:
1998 Helen Drutt: Philadelphia, SOFA: New York; 1997 *Solo Exhibition*, Helen Drutt: Philadelphia; 1994 *In Touch*, Maihaugen, Lillehammer, Norway; 1992 *Design Visions*, Art Gallery of Western Australia, Perth; 1991 Umeleckoprumyslove Muzeum, Prague, Czech Republic; *Solo Exhibition*, Helen Drutt: New York; 1990 *American Dreams, American Extremes*, Museum Het Kruithuis, 's-Hertogenbosch, Netherlands; *Jewelries/Epiphanies*, Artists Foundation Gallery, Boston, MA; 1989 *Infinite Riches*, Museum of Fine Arts, St. Petersburg FL; *Ornamenta 1*, Schmuckmuseum, Pforzheim, Germany; *Schmuckszene '89*, Internationale Handwerksmesse, Munich; 1987 *Wally Gilbert/Thomas Gentille*, Victoria & Albert Museum, London

SELECTED PUBLIC COLLECTIONS:
American Craft Museum, New York; Cooper-Hewitt, National Museum of Design, Smithsonian Institution, New York; Victoria & Albert Museum, London

Photo Credit: Bill Phipps

LAURIE HALL*

BORN:
May 30, 1944, Portland, OR, USA

CURRENT RESIDENCE:
Seattle, WA, USA

SELECTED EXHIBITIONS:
1998 *Torch Songs/ Fifty Years of Northwest Jewelry*, Tacoma Art Museum, Tacoma, WA; 1997 *Hello Again! A New Wave of Recycled Art and Design,* Oakland Museum, CA (traveled); *Urban Interpretations*, Coburn Gallery, The Colorado College, Colorado Springs, CO; 1995 *The Ubiquitous Bead II.*, Bellevue Art Museum, Bellevue, WA; 1994 *I Wood If I Could*, MIA Gallery, Seattle, WA; *A Moveable Feast**, Amsterdam; *Schmuck Unserer Zeit**, Zurich; 1992 *Brilliant Stories: American Narrative Jewelry*, USIS Exhibition Hall, Amman, Jordon (traveled)

SELECTED PUBLIC COLLECTIONS:
King County Arts Collection, Seattle, WA; Washington State Arts Commission, WA

WILLIAM HARPER*

BORN:
June 17, 1944, Bucyrus, OH, USA

CURRENT RESIDENCE:
New York, NY, USA

SELECTED EXHIBITIONS:
1998 *William Harper - Jewelry*, The Society for Arts and Crafts, Boston, MA; 1995 *Body Language*, Cooper-Hewitt, National Design Museum, Smithsonian Institution, New York; *Jewelry From the Permanent Collection*, American Craft Museum, New York; *The White House Collection of American Crafts*, National Museum of American Art, Smithsonian Institute, Washington, D.C.; 1993 *Contemporary Crafts and the Saxe Collection*, Toledo Museum of Art, OH (traveling); *Facet I*, Kunsthal, Rotterdam; 1992 *Of Magic, Power and Memory*, Bellevue Art Museum, WA; 1990 *Collecting for the Future*, Victoria and Albert Museum London

SELECTED PUBLIC COLLECTIONS:
American Craft Museum, New York; The Arkansas Arts Center, Decorative Arts Museum, Little Rock, AK; Columbus Museum of Fine Art, OH; Cooper-Hewitt, National Museum of Design, Smithsonian Institution, New York; The Detroit Institute of Arts, MI; Metropolitan Museum of Art, New York; Minnesota Museum of Art, St. Paul; Mint Museum of Art, Charlotte, NC; Museum of Fine Arts, Boston; Nordenfjeldske Kunstindustrimuseum, Trondheim, Norway; Philadelphia Museum of Art, PA; Renwick Gallery, NMAA, Smithsonian Institution, Washington, DC; Schmuckmuseum, Pforzheim, Germany; The Toledo Museum of Art, OH; The Vatican Museum, Vatican City; Victoria and Albert Museum, London; Walker Hill Art Center Museum, Seoul, Korea; The White House, Washington, D.C.; Yale University Art Gallery, New Haven, CT

JUHANI HEIKKILÄ

BORN:
May 19, 1956, Lahti, Finland

CURRENT RESIDENCE:
Helsinki, Finland

SELECTED EXHIBITIONS:
1998 *Subjects: Narratives '98*, Taideteollisuusmuseo, Helsinki; 1996-97 *Nordic Jewellery Triennal*, Kunstgewerbemuseum, Berlin; Taideteollisuusmuseo, Helsinki; Det Danske Kunstindustrimuseum, Copenhagen (traveled Canada); 1996 *Subjects '96*, Retretti Art Centre, Finland; 1995 *Finnish Design Exhibition*, Museum of Arts, Nice; 1994 *10+10,* Exhibition with Swedish Artists, Västerås Konstmuseum

SELECTED PUBLIC COLLECTIONS:
Taideteollisuusmuseo, Finland; Det Danska Konstindustrimuseum, Copenhagen, Denmark

YASUKI HIRAMATSU

BORN:
April 30, 1926; Osaka Prefecture, Japan

CURRENT RESIDENCE:
Tokyo, Japan

SELECTED EXHIBITIONS:
1998 *Jewellry Moves*, National Museum of Scotland, Edinburgh; 1996 *Schmuck Im Schloss*, Salzburg, Austria; *Solo Exhibition*, The Museum of Arts and Crafts, Itami, Japan; 1995 *The Contemporary Japanese Jewellery Exhibition*, Museum of Decorative Arts, Gent, Belgium; *Contemporary Japanese Studio Crafts*, Victoria and Albert Museum, London; *Crafts in Everyday Life in the 1950s and 1960s*, National Museum of Modern Art, Tokyo; *Solo Exhibition*, Ikeda City Gallery, Ikeda, Osaka Prefecture, Japan; 1994 *Schmuck und Gerät*, Deutsches Goldschmiedehaus, Hanau, Germany (traveled); 1994-1993 *Professor Yasuki Hiramatsu Retirement Exhibition*, Tokyo National University of the Fine Arts and Music

SELECTED PUBLIC COLLECTIONS:
Kumamoto Museum of Traditional Art and Craft, Japan; Museum für Kunst und Gewerbe, Hamburg, Germany; National Museum of Modern Art, Tokyo; Royal Museum of Scotland, Edinburgh; Schmuckmuseum, Pforzheim, Germany; The Imperial Household Agency, Tokyo; Tokyo National University of Fine Arts and Music, Japan; Victoria and Albert Museum, London

RON HO*

BORN:
November 1, 1936, Honolulu, HI, USA

CURRENT RESIDENCE:
Seattle, WA, USA

SELECTED EXHIBITIONS:
1998 *Subjects: Narratives 98*, Taideteollisuusmuseo, Helsinki, Finland; *Torch Songs/ Fifty Years of Northwest Jewelry*, Tacoma Art Museum, Tacoma, WA; 1995 *Becoming Chinese: The Jewelry Art of Ron Ho*, Honolulu Academy of Art, HI; 1994 *A Moveable Feast**, Amsterdam; 1992 *Of Magic, Power and Memory*, Bellevue Art Museum, WA; 1991 *Artists at Work*, Cheney Cowles Museum, Spokane, WA (traveled)

DANIEL JOCZ

BORN:
January 3, 1943, Beloit, WI, USA

CURRENT RESIDENCE:
Cambridge, MA, USA

SELECTED EXHIBITIONS:
1996 *The Gold Show*, American Craft Museum, New York; 1996-97 *Signals: Late Twentieth-Century American Jewelry*, Cranbrook Art Museum, Bloomfield Hills, MI; Montreal Musée des Arts Décoratifs, Quebec; 1993 *Sculptural Concerns: Contemporary American Metal Working*, Fort Wayne Museum of Art, IN (traveled); *Horizons Faculty*, Hudson River Museum, Yonkers, NY; 1992 *Schmuckszene '92*, Internationale Handwerksmesse, Munich; 1991 *Americky Sperk*, Umeleckoprumyslove Muzeum, Prague

SELECTED PUBLIC COLLECTIONS:
American Craft Museum, New York; University of Massachusetts, Amherst

BEPPE KESSLER

BORN:
January 9, 1952, Amsterdam

CURRENT RESIDENCE:
Amsterdam, Netherlands

SELECTED EXHIBITIONS:
1998 *Jewellery Moves,* National Museums of Scotland, Edinburgh; 1996 *Solo Exhibition,* Galerie RA, KunstRai, Amsterdam; *Briljant and well-set,* Nederlands Kostuummuseum, Den Haag; Museum Waterland, Purmerend; 1994 Museum für Kunst und Gewerbe, Hamburg, Germany; 1993 *Voorzien,* Stedelijk Museum, Amsterdam; *Tekens & Ketens,* Museum van der Togt, Amstelveen; Gemeentemuseum, Arnhem, Netherlands; 1992 *Solo Exhibition,* Galerie RA, KunstRai, Amsterdam; 1991 *Bedels aan banden,* Gemeente Museum, Arnhem

SELECTED PUBLIC COLLECTIONS:
Gemeentelijk van Reckummuseum, Apeldoorn, The Netherlands; Gemeente Museum, Arnhem, Netherlands; Nordenfjeldske Kunstindustrimuseum, Trondheim, Norway; Montreal Musée des Arts Décoratifs, Quebec Nederlands Kostuummuseum, Den Haag, Netherlands; Nederlands Textiel Museum, Tilburg; Ísterreichisches Museum für Angewandte Kunst, Vienna; Rijksdienst Beeldende Kunst, Den Haag, Netherlands Stedelijk Museum, Amsterdam

BETSY KING*

BORN:
June 1, 1953, Washington, D.C., USA

CURRENT RESIDENCE:
Ocean City, NJ, USA

SELECTED EXHIBITIONS:
1998 *Subjects: Narratives 98,* Taideteollisuusmuseo, Helsinki, Finland; 1996 *New Jersey Arts Annual: Crafts,* New Jersey State Museum, Trenton, NJ; 1995 *Meet the Artist,* Noyes Museum, Oceanville, NJ; 1994 *Cornucopia of Contemporary Crafts,* Laumeier Sculpture Park, St. Louis, MO; 1992 *Brilliant Stories: American Narrative Jewelry,* USIS Exhibition Hall, Amman, Jordon (traveled); 1990 *Schmuckszene '90,* Internationale Handwerksmesse, Munich; *American Dreams, American Extremes,* Museum Het Kruithuis, 's-Hertogenbosch, Netherlands; *New Jersey Arts Annual: Crafts,* Noyes Museum, Oceanville, NJ

SELECTED PUBLIC COLLECTIONS:
Museum Het Kruithuis, 's-Hertogenbosch, Netherlands

ESTHER KNOBEL*

BORN:
January 14, 1949, Poland

CURRENT RESIDENCE:
Jerusalem, Israel

SELECTED EXHIBITIONS:
1998 *Jewellery Moves*, National Museums of Scotland, Edinburgh; 1996 *Design of the Times: One Hundred Years of the Royal College of Art*, London; 1995 *Solo Exhibition*, Israel Museum, Jerusalem; *Object/Object*, Herzelia Museum of Art; *The Jewell Sign and Symbol*, Kon. Fabiolazaal, Antwerpen, Belgium; 1994 *Esther Knobel: Sketches in Raw Material*, Galerie Ra, Amsterdam; *Local Goddesses*, Tower of David, The Museum of the History of Jerusalem, Israel; 1993 *Holography in Jewellery Design*, Museum für Angewandte Kunst, Köln; *Tekens & Ketens*, Museum van der Togt, Amstelveen; Gemeentemuseum, Arnhem, Netherlands; *Voorzien: Benno Premsela Applied Art Collection*, Stedelijk Museum, Amsterdam

SELECTED PUBLIC COLLECTIONS:
Art Gallery of Western Australia, Perth; Bristol Museum and Art Gallery, Bristol; Cleveland County Museum, Middlesborough, England; Craft board of Australia Council, Sydney; Israel Museum, Jerusalem; Montreal Musée des Arts Décoratifs, Quebec; Museum für Angewandte Kunst, Vienna; Museum Het Kruithuis, 's-Hertogenbosch, Netherlands; Musée des Arts Décoratifs, Paris; National Museum of Modern Art, Kyoto; Stedelijk Museum, Amsterdam

ROBIN KRANITZKY AND KIM OVERSTREET*

KRANITZKY
BORN:
November 10, 1956, Richmond, VA, USA

CURRENT RESIDENCE:
Richmond, VA, USA

OVERSTREET
BORN:
January 29, 1955, Christiansburg, VA, USA

CURRENT RESIDENCE:
Richmond, VA, USA

SELECTED EXHIBITIONS:
1998 *Subjects: Narratives 98*, Taideteollisuusmuseo, Helsinki, Finland; 1997 *Centennial Exhibitions, The Society of Arts and Crafts*, Boston, MA; 1994, 97, 98 *Solo Exhibition*, Helen Drutt: Philadelphia, SOFA: Chicago; 1994 *Desire in Time, Time as Intimacy*, UWM Art Museum, Milwaukee, WI; 1993 *Solo Exhibition*, Helen Drutt: Philadelphia; 1992 *Of Magic, Power and Memory*, Bellevue Art Museum, Bellevue, WA; *Many Mansions, The Art of Shelter*, San Francisco Craft and Folk Art Museum, San Francisco, CA; 1991 *Beauty Is a Story*, Museum Het Kruithuis, 's-Hertogenbosch, Netherlands (traveled); 1990 *American Dreams, American Extremes*, Museum Het Kruithuis, 's-Hertogenbosch, Netherlands

SELECTED PUBLIC COLLECTIONS:
Museum Het Kruithuis, 's-Hertogenbosch, Netherlands; Montreal Musée des Art Décoratifs, Quebec; Renwick Gallery, NMAA, Smithsonian Institution, Washington, D.C.

CATHERINE MARTIN

BORN:
1949, London, England

CURRENT RESIDENCE:
London, England

SELECTED EXHIBITIONS:
1998 *Jewellery Moves,* National Museums of Scotland, Edinburgh; *British Gold/Italian Gold,* Scottish Gallery, Edinburgh; Padua, Italy; Helen Drutt: Philadelphia, SOFA: New York; 1997 *Hipotesi,* Barcelona, Spain; 1995 *Schmuckkunst der Moderne Grossbritannien,* Landesmuseum, Mainz; *Showcase,* Victoria & Albert Museum, London

SELECTED PUBLIC COLLECTIONS:
Victoria & Albert Museum, London; Worshipful Company of Goldsmiths, London; National Museum of Scotland; Birmingham Museums and Art Galleries

RICHARD MAWDSLEY*

BORN:
July 11, 1945, Winfield, KS, USA

CURRENT RESIDENCE:
Canterville, IL, USA

SELECTED EXHIBITIONS:
1996-98 *America's Smithsonian,* In celebration of institution's 150th anniversary (traveling U.S.A.); 1990 *Explorations: The Aesthetic of Excess,* American Craft Museum, New York; 1987 *The Eloquent Object,* The Philbrook Museum of Art, Tulsa, Oklahoma (traveling in U.S.A. and Japan); 1985 *Masterworks of Contemporary American Jewelry: Sources and Concepts,* Victoria and Albert Museum, London

SELECTED PUBLIC COLLECTIONS:
American Craft Museum, New York; Renwick Gallery, National Museum of American Art, Smithsonian Institute, Washington, D.C.; Museum of Fine Arts, Boston, MA, Yale University Art Gallery, New Haven

BRUCE METCALF*

BORN:
September 30, 1949, Amherst, MA, USA

CURRENT RESIDENCE:
Philadelphia, PA, USA

SELECTED EXHIBITIONS:
1998 *Jewellery Moves*, National Museums of Scotland, Edinburgh; *Bridge V: John Garret, Bruce Metcalf, Michael Olszewski*, The Society for Contemporary Crafts, Pittsburgh, PA; *Subjects: Narratives 98*, Taideteollisuusmuseo, Helsinki, Finland; 1997 *Metal Speaks: The Unexpected*, Craft and Folk Art Museum, San Francisco, CA; *Designed for Delight: Alternative Aspects of 20th Century Decorative Arts*, Montreal Musée des Arts Décoratifs, Quebec (traveled); *Celebrating American Craft, 1975-1995*, Det Danske Kunstindustriemuseum, Copenhagen; 1996 *New Times, New Thinking: Jewellery in Europe and America*, Crafts Council, London; National Museum and Gallery, Cardiff, Wales; 1995 *Double Vision*, Charles A. Wustum Museum of Fine Arts, Racine, WI; *Jewelry from the Permanent Collection*, American Craft Museum, New York

SELECTED PUBLIC COLLECTIONS:
American Craft Museum, New York; Cooper-Hewitt, National Museum of Design, Smithsonian Institution, New York; Cranbrook Academy of Art, Bloomfield Hills, MI; Illinois State University, Normal; Montreal Musée des Arts Décoratifs, Quebec; Museum Het Kruithuis, The Netherlands; Philadelphia Museum of Art, PA; Renwick Gallery, NMAA, Smithsonian Institution, Washington, D.C.

LOUIS MUELLER*

BORN:
June 15, 1943, Paterson, NJ, USA

CURRENT RESIDENCE:
Providence, RI, USA

SELECTED EXHIBITIONS:
1997 *Solo Exhibition*, Franklin Parrasch, New York; *Structures-Buildings in American Art; 1900-1997*, John Berggruen Gallery, San Francisco, CA; 1996 *New Times, New Thinking: Jewellery in Europe and America*, Crafts Council, London; National Museum and Gallery, Cardiff, Wales; 1995 *Solo Exhibition*, SOFA: Miami, Jeanine Cox Fine Art, Miami, FL; 1991 *Outdoor Sculpture Festival*, Snug Harbor Cultural Center, Staten Island, NY; 1990 *Rhode Island Sculptors*, Museum of Art, Bristol, RI

SELECTED PUBLIC COLLECTIONS:
American Craft Museum, New York, NY; Museum of Fine Arts, Boston, MA; Philadelphia Museum of Art, PA; The Rhode Island School of Design, Museum of Art, Providence, RI; Victoria and Albert Museum, London

BREON O'CASEY*

BORN:
April 30, 1928, London, England

CURRENT RESIDENCE:
Cornwall, England

SELECTED EXHBITIONS:
1998 *Breon O'Casey: The Last Jewelry Show, In Honor of His 70th Birthday*, Helen Drutt: Philadelphia; 1997 *The Irish Friends of Denis Mitchell*, Bridge Gallery, Dublin; *Breon O'Casey: Mixed Media*, Dartingon Hall, Devon, England; *Solo Exhibition,* Lynn Strover Gallery, Cambridge, England; *Solo Exhibition,* Contemporary Applied Arts; *Cononor Fallon and Breon O'Casey,* Taylor Galleries, Dublin

SELECTED PUBLIC COLLECTIONS:
Arts Council Collection, London, England; Arts Council of Southern Ireland; British Crafts Council, London; Cooper-Hewitt, National Museum of Design, Smithsonian Institution, New York; Craft Council, England; Dartington Hall, Devonshire, England; Granada TV, London; Leeds Museum and Art Gallery, England Arts Council of Northern Ireland, Belfast; Philadelphia Museum of Art, PA; Plymouth Museum and Art Gallery, England; Schmuckmuseum, Pforzheim, Germany; Trinity College, Dublin; Victoria and Albert Museum, London; Worshipful Company of Goldsmiths, London

JUDY ONOFRIO*

BORN:
November 21, 1939, New London, CT, USA

CURRENT RESIDENCE:
Rochester, MN, USA

SELECTED EXHIBITIONS:
1998 *Subjects: Narratives 98*, Taideteollisuusmuseo, Helsinki, Finland; 1996-99 *Pure Vision, American Bead Artists*, (traveling); 1997 *Myths and Magical Fantasies*, California Center for the Arts Museum, Escondido, CA; *American Art Today/The Garden*, Florida International University, Miami, FL; 1996 *Schmuckszene '96*, Internationale Handwerksmesse, Munich; 1995,96,97 *Solo Exhibition*, Leedy Voulkos Gallery, Kansas City, SOFA: Chicago; 1993-97 *Judyland,* Minneapolis Institute of Art, MN; North Dakota Museum of Art, Grand Forks, ND; Laumeier Sculpture Park and Museum, Saint Louis, MO

SELECTED PUBLIC COLLECTIONS:
Arabia Museum, Helsinki, Finland; Cooper-Hewitt, National Museum of Design, Smithsonian Institution, New York; Decorative Arts Museum, Little Rock, AK; Hallmark, Kansas City, MI; Laumeier Sculpture Park and Museum, St. Louis, MON; McKnight Foundation, Minneapolis, MN; The Minneapolis Institute of Art, Minneapolis, MN; Montreal Musée des Arts Décoratifs, Quebec; Museum Het Kruithuis, 's-Hertogenbosch, Netherlands; Taideteollisuusmuseo, Helsinki; North Dakota Museum of Art, Grand Forks, ND; Philadelphia Museum of Art, PA

PAVEL OPOČENSKÝ*

BORN:
August 7, 1954, Karlovy Vary, Czechoslovakia

CURRENT RESIDENCE:
Prague, Czech Republic

SELECTED EXHIBITIONS:
1998 *Jewellery Moves*, National Museums of Scotland, Edinburgh; 1997-98 *Bakelitomanie*, solo exhibition, Galerie Biró, Munich; Galerie Ra, Amsterdam; Jewelerswerk Galerie, Washington, D.C.; Kotelna Galerie, Prague; 1995 *Materia des Loches*, solo exhibition, Galerie Biró, Munich; Helen Drutt: Philadelphia; 1993 *Contemporary Crafts and the Saxe Collection*, Toledo Museum of Art, OH (traveled); 1992 *A Decade of Craft, Recent Acquisitions, Part II*, American Craft Museum, New York; 1990 *American Dreams, American Extremes*, Museum Het Kruithuis, 's-Hertogenbosch, Netherlands

SELECTED PUBLIC COLLECTIONS:
American Craft Musuem, New York; Moravská Galerie, Brno, Czech Republic; Muzeum Ceskeho Rajé, Turnov, Czech Republic; Museum für Kunsthandwerk, Frankfurt a. M.; National Galerie, Bratislava, Slovakia; Turnovshé Museum, Turnov, Czech Republic; Umeleckoprumyslove Muzeum, Prague

RUUDT PETERS*

BORN:
August 17, 1950, Naaldwijk, Netherlands

CURRENT RESIDENCE:
Amsterdam, Netherlands

SELECTED EXHIBITIONS:
1998 *Solo Exhibition*, Jewelerswerk, Washington, D.C., SOFA: New York; 1997 *Lapis*, solo exhibition, Harvard Club of New York; 1996 *New Times, New Thinking: Jewellery in Europe and America*, International Crafts Council, London; National Museum and Gallery, Cardiff, Wales; 1996 *Scanning*, Stedelijk Museum, Amsterdam; *Solo Exhibition*, Gallery Spektrum, Munich; 1995 *European Jewellery Art of the 60s-90s*, Russian Ethnographical Museum, Saint Petersburg

SELECTED PUBLIC COLLECTIONS:
Anger Museum Erfurt, Germany; Cleveland County Museum, Middlesborough, England; Cooper-Hewitt, National Museum of Design, Smithsonian Institution, New York; Danner-Stiftung Collection, Munich; Gemeentemuseum, Arnhem, Museum Boymans van Beuningen, Rotterdam; Museum für Angewandte Kunst, Vienna Museum für Kunst und Gewerbe, Hamburg; Schmuckmuseum, Pforzheim, Germany Stedelijk Museum, Amsterdam; Philadelphia Museum Art, PA; Rijksdienst Beeldende Kunst, Den Haag, Netherlands; Van Reekum Museum, Apeldoorn; Montreal Musée des Arts Décoratifs, Quebec

WENDY RAMSHAW*

BORN:
May 26, 1939, Sunderland, England

CURRENT RESIDENCE:
London, England

SELECTED EXHIBITIONS:
1998 *Jewellery Moves*, National Museums of Scotland, Edinburgh; *Picasso's Ladies,* Victoria and Albert Museum, London, American Craft Museum, New York; 1994 *A Moveable Feast**, Amsterdam; *Schmuck Unserer Zeit**, Zurich; 1993 *Contemporary Jewelry**, Little Rock, AK; *David Watkins/Wendy Ramshaw*, Musée d'Art Moderne et d'Art Contemporaine, Nice; 1992-93 *Korun Kieli**, Gothenburg; Helsinki; 1992 *British Goldsmiths of Today*, Worshipful Company of Goldsmiths, London; *Triennale du Bijou*, Musée du Luxembourg, Paris; 1990 *Collecting for the Future*, Victoria and Albert Museum, London; *Triennale du Bijou*, Musée du Luxembourg, Paris

SELECTED PUBLIC COLLECTIONS:
Australian National Gallery, Canberra; Birmingham City Art Gallery and Museum, England; Contemporary Arts Society, London; Corning Museum of Glass, Corning, New York; Fonds National d'Art Contemporain, Paris; Kunstindustrimuseet i Oslo, Norway; Musée des Arts Décoratifs, Paris; Museum of Modern Art, Kyoto, Japan; National Gallery of Victoria, Melbourne, Australia; National Museum of Modern Art, Kyoto, Japan; National Museum of Whales, Cardiff; Philadelphia Museum of Art, PA; Royal Scottish Museum, Edinburgh; Schmuck-museum, Pforzheim, Germany; Stedelijk Museum, Amsterdam; Victoria and Albert Museum, London; Worshipful Company of Goldsmiths, London

DEBRA RAPOPORT*

BORN:
July 6, 1945, New York, NY, USA

CURRENT RESIDENCE:
New York, NY, USA

SELECTED EXHIBITIONS:
1997 *Trashformations: Recycled Materials in American Art and Design,* Whatcome Museum, Bellingham, WA (traveled); 1994 *A Moveable Feast**, Amsterdam; *Schmuck Unserer Zeit**, Zurich; 1993 *A Head of Fashion: Hats of the 20th Century,* Philadelphia Museum of Art, Philadelphia, PA; *Contemporary Jewelry**, Little Rock, AK; 1992-93 *Korun Kieli**, Gothenburg; Helsinki; 1991 *Passion de Fleurs et de Vegetaux,* Musée des Arts Decoratifs de la Ville de Lausanne, Switzerland

SELECTED PUBLIC COLLECTIONS:
The Metropolitan Museum of Art, New York; Deutsch Foundation, Belmont-sur-Lausanne, Switzerland; Musée des Beaux-Arts, Lausanne

GERD ROTHMANN*

BORN:
January 21, 1941, Frankfurt a. M., Germany

CURRENT RESIDENCE:
Munich, Germany

SELECTED EXHIBITIONS:
1998 *Jewellery Moves*, National Museums of Scotland, Edinburgh; 1997 *Solo Exhibition*, Helen Drutt: Philadelphia, PA; 1994 *A Moveable Feast**, Amsterdam; *Schmuck Unserer Zeit**, Zurich; 1993 *Contemporary Jewelry**, Little Rock, AK; *Müncher Goldschmiede*, Stadtmuseum, Munich; *Schmuckmassnhmen*, Goldschmiedhaus, Hanau; 1992-93 *Korun Kieli**, Gothenburg; Helsinki; 1992 *Neoteric Jewelry*, Snug Harbor Cultural Center, Staten Island, NY (traveled); 1991 *Europäisches Kunsthandwerk*, Haus der Wirtschaft, Stuttgart; 1990 *Danner Preis '90*, Danner-Stiftung, Munich; *Signaturen*, Stadtischen Museum, Schwäbisch Gmünd, Germany

SELECTED PUBLIC COLLECTIONS:
Danner-Stiftung Collection, Munich; Deutsches Goldschmiedehaus, Hanau, Germany; Landesmuseum, Oldenburg, Germany; Müncher Stadtmuseum, Munich; Museum für Angewandte Kunst, Vienna; Museum für Kunst und Gewerbe, Hamburg; Museum of Modern Art, New York; National Museum of Modern Art, Tokyo; Schmuckmuseum, Pforzheim, Germany; Stedelijk Museum, Amsterdam; Victoria and Albert Museum, London

MARGARETH SANDSTRÖM

BORN:
June 2, 1950, Norrköping, Sweden

CURRENT RESIDENCE:
Linköping, Sweden

SELECTED EXHIBITIONS:
1998 *Kraft & Art*, Hemslöjdsgården, Linköping, Sweden; 1996-97 *Nordic Jewellery Triennal*, Kunstgewerbemuseum, Berlin; Det Danske Kunstindustrimuseum, Copenhagen (traveled); 1996 *Du Contemporain, Bijoux et Orfevrerie de créateurs*, Les Musées de Cagnes-Sur-Mer, Côte d'Azur, France; 1995 *Ädla Tendenser-Framtidens Fornform*, Historiska Museum, Stockholm, Sweden; 1993-95 *Silver till Nytta och Lust*, National Museum, Stockholm; Kulturen i Lund, Sweden (traveled)

SELECTED PUBLIC COLLECTIONS:
Nationalmuseum, Stockhom, Sweden; Länsmuseum, Linköping, Sweden; Kulturen, Lund, Sweden

LUCY SARNEEL

BORN:
March 4, 1961, Maastricht, Netherlands

CURRENT RESIDENCE:
Amsterdam, Netherlands

SELECTED EXHIBITIONS:
1996 *Verlicht en Getooid*, K.C.B., Bergen, Netherlands; 1995 *Sieraad, Symbool, Signaal,* Kon. Fabila-saal, Antwerpen, Belgium; 1994 *Sign of Mine*, Museum für Angewandte Kunst, Keulin, Quitsland; 1993 *Facet I*, KunstHal, Rotterdam, Netherlands; *Tekens & Ketens*, Museum van der Togt, Amstelveen; Gemeentemuseum, Arnhem, Netherlands; 1991 *Beauty is a Story,* Museum Het Kruithuis, 's-Hertogenbosch, Netherlands; 1990 *Triénnale du Bijou*, Musée du Luzembourg, Paris, France

SELECTED PUBLIC COLLECTIONS:
Museum Het Kruithuis, 's-Hertogenbosch; Museum voor Moderne Kunst, Arnhem; Van Reekummuseum, Apeldoorn; Stedelijk Museum, Amsterdam;Nederlands Textielmuseum, Tilburg; Haags Gemeentemuseum, Den Haag; Montreal Musée des Arts Décoratifs, Quebec

MARJORIE SCHICK*

BORN:
August 29, 1941, Taylorville, IL, USA

CURRENT RESIDENCE:
Pittsburgh, KS, USA

SELECTED EXHIBITIONS:
1998 *Jewellery Moves*, National Museums of Scotland, Edinburgh; *Marjorie Schick: A Sense of Place,* Galerie RA, Amsterdam; 1997 *Celebrating American Craft 1975-1995*, Det Danske Kunstindustriemuseum, Copenhagen, Denmark; 1996 *Schmuckszene '96*, Internationale Handwerksmesse, Munich; *New Times, New Thinking: Jewellery in Europe and America,* International Crafts Council, London; National Museum and Gallery, Cardiff, Wales; 1995 *Jewelry from the Permanent Collection*, American Craft Museum, New York

SELECTED PUBLIC COLLECTIONS:
American Craft Museum, New York; Kunstindustrimuseet i Oslo, Norway; Cleveland County Museum, Cleveland, England; Indiana University Fine Arts Museum, Bloomington; John Michael Kohler Art Center, Sheboygan, WI; Gemeentelijke van Reekummuseum, Apeldoorn, Netherlands; Nordenfjeldske Kunstindustrimuseum, Trondheim, Norway; The National Museum of Contemporary Art, Seoul, South Korea; The National Museum of Modern Art, Kyoto, Japan; Renwick Gallery, NMAA, Smithsonian Institution, Washington, D.C.; Victoria and Albert Museum, London, England

BERNHARD SCHOBINGER*

BORN:
January 18, 1946, Zurich, Switzerland

CURRENT RESIDENCE:
Richterswil, Switzerland

SELECTED EXHIBITIONS:
1997 *Gioielli di fine millenio*, Fattidarte, Piacenza, Italy; 1996 New Times, *New Thinking: Jewellery in Europe and America*, Crafts Council, London; National Museum and Gallery, Cardiff, Wales; 1994 *A Moveable Feast**, Amsterdam; *Schmuck Unserer Zeit**, Zurich; 1993 *Contemporary Jewelry**, Little Rock, AK; *Facet I,* Kunsthal, Rotterdam; 1992-93 *Korun Kieli**, Gothenburg; Helsinki; 1991 *Neoteric Jewellery*, Snug Harbor Cultural Center, Staten Island, NY; 1990 *Zeitgenössisches deutsches Kunsthandwerk*, C. Vögele, Museum für Kunsthandwerk, Frankfurt a.M.

SELECTED PUBLIC COLLECTIONS:
Grassimuseum, Leipzig, Germany; Landesmuseum, Stuttgart Hiko Mizuno College, Tokyo; Kunsthaus Aarau; Museum für Angewandte Kunst, Munich; Royal College of Art, London; Sammlung Schweizerische Eidgenossenschaft; Seedammkulturzentrum, Pfaffikon, Switzerland; Stedelijk Museum, Amsterdam; Württembergisches, Landesmuseum, Stuttgart

DEGANIT SCHOCKEN*

BORN:
November 21, 1947, Kibbutz Amir, Israel

CURRENT RESIDENCE:
Jerusalem, Israel

SELECTED EXHIBITIONS:
1998 *Solo Exhibition,* Helen Drutt: Philadelphia; 1996 *Solo Exhibition*, Galerie Ra, Amsterdam, Netherlands; *Women/Beyond Borders* (traveling World Exhibition, USA, Israel); 1994 Israeli Contemporary Crafts, The National Museum of Art, Tokyo, Japan; *Local Goddesses,* Tower of David, The Museum of the History of Jerusalem, Jerusalem, Israel; 1992 *Triennale du Bijou,* Musée des Arts Décoratifs, Paris; *Stone - Touch - Jewelry,* The Oppenheimer Diamond Museum, Ramat Gan, Israel; 1990 *Triennale du Bijou*, Musée de Luxembourg, Paris, France; *Signaturen,* Stadtischen Museum, Schwäbisch Gmünd, Germany

SELECTED PUBLIC COLLECTIONS:
The Brooklyn Museum, New York; Israel Museum Jerusalem; Nordenfjeldske Kunstindustrimuseum, Trondheim, Norway

JOYCE J. SCOTT*

BORN:
November 15, 1948, Baltimore, MD, USA

CURRENT RESIDENCE:
Baltimore, MD, USA

SELECTED EXHIBITIONS:
1998 *Jewellery Moves*, National Museums of Scotland, Edinburgh; *Centennial Exhibition: Fiber*, The Society of Arts and Craft, Boston, MA; 1997 *Celebrating American Craft, 1975-1995*, Det Danske Kunstindustriemuseum, Copenhagen; *Stitchers and Beaders, America's Best*, The Ohio Craft Museum, Columbus; *Strung, Woven, Knitted and Sewn: Beadwork form Europe, Africa, Asia and the Americas*, Milwaukee Art Museum, Milwaukee, WI; 1996 *Breaking Barriers, Recent American Craft*, American Craft Museum, New York; *The Ubiquitous Bead II and The Rebellious Bead*, Bellevue Museum of Art, WA; 1995 *Elizabeth T. Scott and Joyce J. Scott*, Tubman African American Museum, Macon, GA; *Relatively Speaking/Mothers and Daughters in Art,* Snug Harbor Cultural Center, Staten Island, NY

SELECTED PUBLIC COLLECTIONS:
Baltimore Museum of Art, MD; The Detroit Institute of Arts, MI; Mint Museum, Winston-Salem, NC; Musée des Arts Décoratifs, Montreal; Museum Het Kruithuis, 's-Hertogenbosch, Netherlands; Pennsylvania Convention Center Authority, Philadelphia, PA; Philbrook Museum of Art, Tulsa, OK; Philadelphia Museum of Art, PA; Spirit Square Center of the Arts, Charlotte, NC

BARBARA SEIDENATH

BORN:
July 29, 1960, Munich, Germany

CURRENT RESIDENCE:
Providence, RI, USA

SELECTED EXHIBITIONS:
1998 *Solo Exhibition*, Galerie Slavik, Vienna; 1996 *Schmuckschau,* Internationale Handwerksmesse, Munich; *Dannerpreis '96,* Neue Sammlung, Munich; *Gold and Silver*, American Craft Museum, New York; 1995 *International Enamel Exhibition*, Coburg, Germany; 1994 *Was Ihr Wollt,* Badisches Landesmuseum, Karlsruhe, Germany; 1993 *Müncher Goldschmiede*, Stadtmuseum, Munich; *Dannerpreis '93*, Bamberg, Germany; *Exhibition with Irmgard Zeitler,* Gallery Slavik, Vienna; *Förderpreis '93, Vorschläge der Jury,* Lothringerstr., Munich; 1992 *Neoteric Jewelry*, Snug Harbor Cultural Center, Staten Island, NY (traveled); 1990 Museum der dtsch. Porzellan Industrie, Hohenberg, Germany

STEPHAN SEYFFERT*

BORN:
August 6, 1960, Kaiserslautern, Germany

CURRENT RESIDENCE:
Karlsruhe, Germany

SELECTED EXHIBITIONS:
1998 *Jewellery Moves,* National Museums of Scotland, Edinburgh; *A Matter of Materials,* Metropolis Gallery, Seattle; Prime Gallery, Toronto; Musée des Arts Décoratifs, Montreal; 1997 *Jewellery in Past, Present and Future,* Crafts Victoria Gallery, Melbourne

SONDRA SHERMAN

BORN:
October 21, 1958, Philadelphia, PA, USA

CURRENT RESIDENCE:
Savannah, GA, USA

SELECTED EXHIBITIONS:
1996 *New Times, New Thinking: Jewellery in Europe and America,* Crafts Council, London; National Museum and Gallery, Cardiff, Wales; *Signals: Late Twentieth-Century American Jewelry,* Cranbrook Art Museum, Bloomfield Hills, MI; Montreal Musée des Arts Décoratifs, Quebec; *Schmuckszene '96,* Internationale Handwerksmesse, Munich; Susan Cummins Gallery, Miami, FL, SOFA: Miami; 1995,96 Jewelerswerk Galerie, SOFA: Chicago

HELEN SHIRK*

BORN:
January 25, 1942, Buffalo, NY, USA

CURRENT RESIDENCE:
La Mesa, CA, USA

SELECTED EXHIBITIONS:
1998 *Revelations: New Jewelry from SNAG,* The Society for Contemporary Crafts, Pittsburgh, PA; 1997 *Silver Servers: The Rabinovitch Collection,* Goldsmiths' Hall, London; *American Masters of Late 20th Century Holloware,* Georgia Museum of Art, Athens, GA; *Celebrating American Craft 1975-1995,* Det Danske Kunstindustriemuseum, Copenhagen, Denmark; 1995 *Helen Shirk: Contemporary Jewelry 1970-1995,* Helen Drutt: Philadelphia, PA; 1994 *A Moveable Feast*,* Amsterdam; *Schmuck Unserer Zeit*,* Zurich; 1993 *Corpus: Norwegian and International Craft Art,* Vestlandske Kunstindustrimuseum, Bergen, Norway

SELECTED PUBLIC COLLECTIONS:
American Craft Museum, New York; Carnegie Museum of Art, Pittsburgh, PA; Contemporary Museum, Honolulu, HI; Marietta College, Marietta, OH; Minnesota Museum of Art, St. Paul, MN; Memphis Brooks Museum of Art, Memphis, TN; National Museum of Art, Kyoto, Japan; Oakland Museum of Art, Oakland, CA; Philadelphia Museum of Art, PA; Renwick Gallery, NMAA, Smithsonian Institution, Washington, D.C.; Schmuckmuseum, Pforzheim, Germany; University of Texas, El Paso, TX; Victoria and Albert Museum, London

JIŘÍ ŠIBOR

BORN:
April 15, 1966, Brno, Czechoslovakia

CURRENT RESIDENCE:
Brno, Czech Republic

SELECTED EXHIBITIONS:
1998 *Jewellery Moves,* National Museums of Scotland, Edinburgh; 1997-98 *Czech Modern Jewelry in Stríbro,* Stríbro, Czech Republic; New City Hall, Prague; Museum of Glass and Jewelry, Jablonec nad Nisou, Czech Republic (traveled); 1997 Helen Drutt: Philadelphia, Jewelers' Werk, Washington, D.C., SOFA: Chicago; *Schmuckszene '97,* Internationale Handwerksmesse, Munich; 1996 *Der Moment des Schmucks,* solo exhibition, Gallery Biró, Munich, Germany; 1995-96 *Between Ornament and Function,* Moravian Gallery, Brno, Czech Republic; North Bohemian Museum, Liberec, Czech Republic; 1995 *Symposium and Workshop of Jewelry in Smrzovka,* Museum of Glass and Jewelry, Jablonec nad Nisou, Czech Republic

SELECTED PUBLIC COLLECTIONS:
Moravian Gallery, Museum of Applied Arts, Brno, Czech Republic

PETER SKUBIC*

BORN:
August 11, 1935, Gornji-Milanovac, Yugoslavia

CURRENT RESIDENCE:
St. Michael, Austria

SELECTED EXHIBITIONS:
1996 *Solo Exhibition*, Galerie Slavik, Vienna; 1995 *Der Kosmos des Peter Skubic*, Grassi-Museum, Leipzig; Museum für Angewandte Kunst, Köln; 1993 *Without Guarantee*, solo exhibition, Galerie Spektrum, Munich; *Facet I*, Kunsthal, Rotterdam; 1992 *Neoteric Jewelry*, Snug Harbor Cultural Center, Staten Island, NY (traveled); *Triennale du Bijou*, Musée des Arts Décoratifs, Paris; 1991 *Capitales Europeannes du Nouveau Design*, Centre George Pompidou, Paris; *KölnKunst*, Kunsthalle, Köln; 1990 *Triennale du Bijou*, Musée du Luxembourg, Paris

SELECTED PUBLIC COLLECTIONS:
Anger-Museum, Erfurt; Badisches Landesmuseum, Karlsruhe, Germany; Bundesministerium für Unterricht und Kunst, Vienna; Kunstgewerbemuseum, Berlin; Kunstgewerbemuseum, Jablonec; Landesmuseum, Klagenfurt; Müncher Stadmuseum, Munich; Museum Boymans-van Beuningen, Rotterdam; Museum des 20.Jahrhunderts, Vienna; Museum für Angewandte Kunst, Vienna; Museum für Kunst und Gewerbe, Hamburg National Museum of Modern Art, Kyoto; Muzeum Ceskeho Raje, Turnov, Czech Republic; Neue Galerie, Museum für Moderne Kunst, Linz, Austria; Neue Galerie, Sammlung Ludwig, Aachen; Neue Sammlung, Museum für Angewandte Kunst, Munich; Schmuckmuseum Pforzheim, Germany

KIFF SLEMMONS*

BORN:
October 18, 1944, Maxton, NC, USA

CURRENT RESIDENCE:
Seattle, WA, USA

SELECTED EXHIBITIONS:
1998 *Subjects: Narratives 98*, Taideteollisuusmuseo, Helsinki, Finland; *Torch Songs/ Fifty Years of Northwest Jewelry*, Tacoma Art Museum, Tacoma, WA; *Metalcraft*, Western Washington University; Boise Art Museum; 1997 *Cuts and Repose*, solo exhibition, Susan Cummins Gallery, Mill Valley, CA; *Metal Speaks: The Unexpected*, Craft and Folk Art Museum, San Francisco, CA; *Trashformations: Recycled Materials in American Art and Design*, Whatcome Museum, Bellingham, WA (traveled); *In the Beginning Was the Word*, Charles A. Wustum Museum of Fine Arts, Racine, WI; *Hello Again! A New Wave of Recycled Art and Design*, Oakland Museum, CA; 1995, 97 *Solo Exhibition*, Susan Cummins Gallery, Mill Valley, CA; 1996 *Schmuckszene'95*, Internationale Handwerksmesse, Munich; 1994 *Solo Exhibition*, Mobilia Gallery, Cambridge, MA

ROBERT SMIT*

BORN:
March 29, 1941, Delft, Netherlands

CURRENT RESIDENCE:
Amsterdam, Netherlands

SELECTED EXHIBITIONS:
1998 *Jewellery Moves,* National Museums of Scotland, Edinburgh; 1997 *De Bruiloftsreportage,* Tekeningen Centraal Museum, Utrecht, Netherlands; *Gioielli di fine millenio,* Fattidarte, Piacenza, Italy; 1996-97 *7. Erfurter Schmucksymposium,* Angermuseum-Barfusserkirche, Erfurt (traveled); 1998 *Kortsluiting,* solo exhibition, Galerie Louise Smit, Amsterdam; 1996 *Scanning,* Stedelijk Museum, Amsterdam; *Design and Identity, Aspects of European Design,* Louisiana, Museum of Modern Art, Humblebaek, Denmark

SELECTED PUBLIC COLLECTIONS:
Danner-Stiftung, Munich, Germany; Centraal Museum, Utrecht, Netherlands; Haags Gemeente Museum, Den Haag, Netherlands; Gemeente Museum, Arnhem, Netherlands; Museum Het Kruithuis, 's-Hertogenbosch, Netherlands Rijksdienst Beeldende Kunst, Den Haag, Netherlands; Schmuckmuseum Reuchlinhaus, Pforzheim, Germany; Stedelijk Museum, Amsterdam; Stedelijk Museum Het Prinsenhof, Delft, Netherlands; Van Reekum Museum, Apeldoorn, Netherlands

RAMONA SOLBERG

BORN:
May 10, 1921, Watertown, SD, USA

CURRENT RESIDENCE:
Seattle, WA, USA

SELECTED EXHIBITIONS:
1998 *Torch Songs/ Fifty Years of Northwest Jewelry,* Tacoma Art Museum, Tacoma, WA; 1993 *Documents Northwest, The Poncho Series: Six Jewelers,* Seattle Art Museum, WA; *Lifetime Achievements*: The ACC College of Fellows in Metal, National Ornamental Metal Museum, Memphis, TN; 1992 *Of Magic Power and Memory,* Bellevue Art Museum, WA

SELECTED PUBLIC COLLECTIONS:
American Craft Museum, New York; Jacksonville Art Museum, Jacksonville, FL; King County Arts Commission, Seattle, WA; Renwick Gallery, NMAA, Smithsonian Institution, Washington, DC

BETTINA SPECKNER

BORN:
1962, Offenburg, Germany

CURRENT RESIDENCE:
Munich, Germany

SELECTED EXHIBITIONS:
1998 *Schmuckszene '98,* Internationale Handwerksmesse, Munchen; 1997 *Sonderschau des Bayerischen Kunstgewerbeverein,* Handwerksmesse, Munich; 1996 *Danner Preis '96,* Neue Sammlung, Munich; SOFA: Chicago, IL; 1995 *Solo Exhibition,* Galerie Spektrum, Munich; *Schmuckszene '95,* Internationale Handwerksmesse, Munich

SELECTED PUBLIC COLLECTIONS:
Danner-Stiftung Collection, Munich; Neue Sammlung, Munich; Stadtmuseum, Munich

TORE SVENSSON

BORN:
February 10, 1948, Alfta, Sweden

CURRENT RESIDENCE:
Gothenburg, Sweden

SELECTED EXHIBITIONS:
1997 *Swedish Contemporary Craft Art* (traveling in Japan); 1996-97 *Nordic Jewellery Triennal,* Kunstgewerbemuseum, Berlin; Det Danske Kunstindustrimuseum, Copenhagen (traveled); 1996 Hjörring Konstmuseum, Hjörring, Denmark; 1994-95 *Nordic Images* (traveling in Nordic countries); 1994 Vestlandske Kunstindustrimuseum, Bergen, Norway; 1992 Kunstlerzentrum, Lübeck, Germany

SELECTED PUBLIC COLLECTIONS:
National Museum, Stockholm, Sweden; Rhösska Museet, Gothenburg, Sweden

DETLEF THOMAS

BORN:
June 22, 1959, Dormagen, Germany

CURRENT RESIDENCE:
Bremen, Germany

SELECTED EXHIBITIONS:
1998 *Micro Organism,* Wooster Gardens, New York; *Solo Exhibition,* Galerie Slavik, Vienna; 1996 *Solo Exhibition,* Angermuseum, Erfurt; *Jewellery in Europe and America,* Crafts Council, London; 1995 *Solo Exhibition,* Jewelerswerk Gallery, Washington D.C.; 1994 *Solo Exhibition,* Musikhochschule, Munich 1993 *Facet I,* Kunsthalle, Rotterdam; *Solo Exhibition,* Galerie Slavik, Vienna; 1991 *Beauty is a Story,* Museum Het Kruithuis, 's-Hertogenbosch, Netherlands, (traveled); *Neoteric Jewellery,* Snug Harbor Cultural Center, Staten Island, NY; 1990 *Triennale du Bijou,* Musée du Luxembourg, Paris

SELECTED PUBLIC COLLECTIONS:
Angermuseum, Erfurt; Danner-Stiftung Collection, Munich; Musée des Arts Décorativs, Paris; Museum Het Kruithuis, 's-Hertogenbosch, Netherlands; Neue Sammlung, Munich; Royal College of Art, London; Schmuckmuseum, Pforzheim, Germany

MERRILY TOMPKINS*

BORN:
August 29, 1947, Everet, WA, USA

CURRENT RESIDENCE:
Ellensburg, WA, USA

SELECTED EXHIBITIONS:
1998 *Torch Songs/ Fifty Years of Northwest Jewelry,* Tacoma Art Museum, Tacoma, WA; *Setting the Stage,* Washington State Convention and Trade Center Gallery, Seattle, WA; 1995 *Sex and Satan,* Two Bells Tavern, Seattle, WA; 1994 *Eyes on Public Art: Points of View,* Public Locations, Seattle, WA; *A Moveable Feast*,* Amsterdam; Schmuck Unserer Zeit*, Zurich

SELECTED PUBLIC COLLECTIONS:
Seattle Portable Works Collection

KAREL VOTIPKA

BORN:
1964, Czechoslovakia

CURRENT RESIDENCE:
Melnik, Czech Republic

SELECTED EXHIBITIONS:
1998 *Ceský moderin sperk*, Galerie Vartai, Vilnius, Latvia; Museum skla a biéuterie, Jablonec n. Nisou; *Sta roméstkß radnice*, Ceské Budejovice; *Solo Exhibition*, Galerie Kotelna, Prague; 1995 *Solo Exhibition*, Galerie U sv. Martina, Prague 1994 *Solo Exhibition*, Galerie Klarinet, Prague

SELECTED PUBLIC COLLECTIONS:
Národni muzeum v Praze

PETER DE WIT*

BORN:
September 29, 1952, Leiden, Netherlands

CURRENT RESIDENCE:
Linköping, Sweden

SELECTED EXHIBITIONS:
1998 *Kraft & Art*, Hemslöjdsgõrden, Linköping, Sweden; 1996-97 *Nordic Jewellery Triennal*, Kunstgewerbemuseum, Berlin; Det Danske Kunstindustrimuseum, Copenhagen (traveled); 1995 *Ädla Tendenser-Framtidens Fornform*, Historiska Museum, Stockholm, Sweden; 1993-95 *Silver till Nytta och Lust*, National Museum, Stockholm; Kulturen i Lund, Sweden (traveled); 1992 *Triennale du Bijou*, Museé des Arts Décoratifs, Paris, France; 1991 *Solo Exhibition*, Oskarshamn Konsthall, Oskarshamn, Sweden; *Schmuckszene '91*, Internationale Handwerksmesse, Munich; 1990 *N.F.S.*, Röhsska Museet, Gothenburg, Sweden

SELECTED PUBLIC COLLECTIONS:
Det Danske Konstindustrimuseum, Copenhagen, Denmark; Kunstgewerbemuseum, Berlin, Germany; Linköpings Länsmuseum, Linköping, Sweden; Museum für Angewandte Kunst, Vienna; Nationalmuseum, Stockholm, Sweden; Nederlands Kunststichting, Amsterdam, Netherlands; Nordenfjeldske Kunstindustrimuseum, Trondheim, Norway; Rijksdienst Beeldende Kunst, Den Haag, Netherlands; Röhsska Museet, Gothenburg, Sweden

MARGARET WEST*

BORN:
August 31, 1936, Melbourne, Australia

CURRENT RESIDENCE:
Sydney, NSW, Australia

SELECTED EXHIBITIONS:
1997 *Notes: Jewellery & Other Objects*, Crawford Gallery, Sydney, NSW; 1994 *A Moveable Feast**, Amsterdam; *Schmuck Unserer Zeit**, Zurich; 1992-94 *Interstices: Works by Margaret West*, Art Gallery of Western Australia; *Artspace,* Sydney; Jam Factory, Adelaide; Canberra School of Art Gallery; 1993 *Contemporary Jewelry**, Little Rock, AK; *The Art of Jewellery*, Setgaya Art Museum, Tokyo; 1987-88 *Four Woman Exhibition*, National Gallery of Victoria, Melbourne; The Craft Gallery, Ontario Crafts Council, Toronto; San Diego State University, CA; *The Houston International Festival*, TX

SELECTED PUBLIC COLLECTIONS:
Australia Council, Crafts Board National Art Gallery, Canberra; National Gallery of Victoria, Melbourne; Power House Museum, Sydney; Royal Melbourne Institute of Technology; Queen Victoria Museum and Art Gallery, Launceston, Tasmania; Queensland Art Gallery, Brisbane, Australia; South Australian Art Gallery; Victorian Ministry for the Arts; Art Gallery of Western Australia, Perth

NANCY WORDEN

BORN:
November 29, 1954, Boston, MA, USA

CURRENT RESIDENCE:
Seattle, WA, USA

SELECTED EXHIBITIONS:
1998 *Torch Songs/ Fifty Years of Northwest Jewelry,* Tacoma Art Museum, Tacoma, WA; *Solo Exhibition,* Traver-Sulton Gallery, Seattle, WA; 1997 *Food, Glorious Food: Artists and Eating,* Charles A. Wustum Museum of Fine Arts, Racine, WI; *Craft as Art - Art as Craft,* Katonah Museum of Art, Katonah, NY; *In the Beginning Was the Word,* Charles A. Wustum Museum of Fine Arts, Racine, WI; 1996 *Just Add Water: Artists and The Aqueous World,* Charles A. Wustum Museum of Fine Arts, Racine, WI; *Ubiquitous Bead II,* Bellevue Art Museum, Bellevue, WA; 1995 *Jewelry from the Permanent Collection,* American Craft Museum, New York, NY

SELECTED PUBLIC COLLECTIONS:
American Craft Museum, New York, NY; City of Seattle Seattle Art Museum, WA; The University of Georgia, Athens, GA

* **EXHIBITED:**
MODERN JEWELRY 1964-1984: PHILADELPHIA MUSEUM OF ART, PA, 1986/1987; CLEVELAND INSTITUTE OF ART, OH 1986; HONOLULU ACADEMY OF ART, HI, 1986; MONTREAL MUSÉE DES ARTS DÉCORATIFS, 1984/1985 - KORUN KIELI (THE LANGUAGE OF JEWELRY) 1964-1992: 1992/1993 RÖHSSKA KONSTSLÖJDMUSEET, GOTHENBURG; TAIDETEOLLISUUSMUSEO, 1992 - CONTEMPORARY JEWELRY 1964-1993: THE ARKANSAS ARTS CENTER, LITTLE ROCK, AK, 1993 - SCHMUCK UNSERER ZEIT 1964-1994: MUSEUM BELLERIVE, ZURICH, 1994 - A MOVABLE FEAST 1964-1994: MUSEUM VOOR MODERNE KUNST, OSTEND, 1995; STEDELIJK MUSEUM, AMSTERDAM, 1994/1995

Brooching It diplomatically.
A Tribute To
Madeleine K. Albright

HELEN W. DRUTT ENGLISH
Einleitung

"Wenn ich gefragt würde … worauf die einzigartige Prosperität und die wachsende Stärke dieses Volkes (der Amerikaner) hauptsächlich zurückzuführen wäre, würde ich antworten: Auf die Überlegenheit seiner Frauen."

Alexis de Tocqueville
Über die Demokratie in Amerika

"Man wird nicht als Frau geboren, man wird zur Frau."

Simone de Beauvoir
Das andere Geschlecht

Adler, ein Zylinder, Schlangen, Bienen, Luftballons, Spinnen und das Kapitol sprangen dem Leser unter der Überschrift "Brooching it Diplomatically" ins Auge. Es handelte sich dabei um einen Artikel im *Time Magazine* vom 27. März 1997 über eine ungewöhnliche Strategie der Madeleine K. Albright, der ersten Frau in der amerikanischen Geschichte, die den Posten der Außenministerin innehat. Der Artikel beschäftigte sich mit der Vielfalt der Botschaften, die Madeleine Albright durch die Broschen, die sie trägt, vermittelt und die Ansichten, die sie damit verkündet. Ich sprühte vor Begeisterung, als ich an die Künstler dachte, die die Herausforderung eingehen könnten, eine einzigartige Brosche für eine Frau in ihrer Position zu entwerfen.

Die Idee war geboren, und damit begannen die Vorbereitungen. Die Verständigung mit Künstlern in der ganzen Welt, ganz zu schweigen vom Außenministerium, war ein schwieriges Unterfangen. Ich schrieb einen Brief an die Außenministerin und brachte darin meinen Wunsch zum Ausdruck, eine Ausstellung zu organisieren, die ihrem gezielten Einsatz von Broschen Tribut zollen sollte. Ihr Büro wurde in den folgenden Monaten über die weiteren Entwicklungen auf dem laufenden gehalten. In den achtzehn Monaten nach Erscheinen des *Time*-Artikels wurden 74 Einladungen versandt, 61 Künstler aus sechzehn Ländern antworteten mit 71 Arbeiten, die sich sowohl durch ihre Kreativität und ihren Einfallsreichtum als auch durch Humor, Ironie und Patriotismus auszeichnen. Neun Broschen wurden nicht eigens für dieses Projekt entworfen, die Künstler waren jedoch der Meinung, daß diese Objekte dem Thema durchaus angemessen seien. Sie alle erhellen die glaubwürdige Aussagekraft von Schmuck als Anmerkung zur Geschichte.

Schmuck ist die persönlichste Ausdrucksform der Kunst, und seine innige Verbindung zum Menschen kann man nicht umgehen. Die Kunstobjekte dieser Ausstellung sind dafür gedacht, als Symbol der Stellung, als Ehrenzeichen, als Zeichen ritueller Erfahrung oder zur reinen Zierde getragen zu werden (und nicht, um in einer Schublade oder einem Schmuckkästchen versteckt zu werden). Sie bilden eine sichtbare Verbindung zwischen dem Künstler, dem Träger und dem Publikum, die eine geistige Einheit schafft. Im Fall von Madeleine K. Albright wird diese Identifikation durch ein internationales, öffentliches Forum erweitert. Wohl wissend um ihre Position der Macht, stellt sie ihre Sensibilität auf die Probe. Sie vertraut offensichtlich ihrem Instinkt und hat das Vertrauen, der ganzen Welt ihren Verhandlungsstandpunkt durch ihre Broschen anzuzeigen.

Das Magazin *George* stellte fest, daß ein auf einer Perle sitzender Freiheitsadler zur "Brosche der Sicherheit" in den politischen und diplomatischen Kreisen der Hauptstadt Washington geworden ist. Es ist unser Bestreben, daß diese Ausstellung aus voller Kehle "Bye Bye Birdie" für die "Sicherheitsnadel" singt. Hier richten wir uns nach der Ministerin selbst, die in der Zeitung *Newsweek* (vom 5. November 1997) bemerkte: "Wenn wir unsere Ansichten und Interessen respektiert sehen wollen, können wir uns nicht am Spielfeldrand aufhalten ...". Ebenso können wir den vergoldeten, gußeisernen Adler nicht unangefochten fliegen lassen, wenn es Scharen von Künstlern gibt, die voller kreativer Ideen stecken:

Laurie Halls Schmuckstück *Cutting* trägt das Wort "Conscience" auf einer Silberschere, um eindringlich eine "sensible Betrachtungsweise von Fairneß und Gerechtigkeit" einzuschärfen, ein einfaches "VIP" von Ramona Solberg grüßt die herausragende Stellung von Madeleine K. Albright, und Nancy Wordens *Arms Agreement* ist eine visuelle Erinnerung daran, daß Madeleine Albrights Händeschütteln "eine Geste der Freundlichkeit und des guten Willens" ist. Merrily Tompkins Brosche ruft die Außenministerin auf, ihre Position zu nutzen, um die Verstümmelung weiblicher Genitalien zu mißbilligen, während Louis Mueller hofft, daß der Schriftzug "Subscribe" – dem *ARTFORUM* entnommen – die Welt daran erinnert, die Künste zu unterstützen. Esther Knobels *Kisses from Jerusalem* sehen wie Miniaturfeuerbomben aus, bestehend aus einem Set mehrdeutiger Ornamente. Sie stehen in völligem Kontrast zur klassischen Form von Yasuki Hiramatsus Goldbrosche, die die Harmonie der fünf Erdteile wiedergibt und seinen Wunsch nach Weltfrieden symbolisiert. Ron Ho bezieht sich auf seine Abstammung von chinesischen Großeltern, um Madeleine K. Albrights Präsenz und Stellung in Form eines Drachens zu symbolisieren, der "Macht und Weisheit" repräsentiert. Karel Votipkas postmoderne Broschenkonstruktion feiert einen amerikanischen Wolkenkratzer mit zwei angrenzenden Türmen, die die Nachbarstaaten Mexiko und Kanada darstellen. Thomas Gentilles Aluminiumquadrat, das in der Reinheit seiner Form präzise gearbeitet ist, Peter de Wits Kopie des *Washington Monument* aus Kristall und wertvollen Edelsteinen und Barbara Seidenaths geometrische Form mit eingelegten Diamanten stellen weitere Schmuckkonstruktionen dar. Daniel Joczs erzählender *Punch* in Goldrelief spielt auf den diplomatischen Austausch von verbalen Schlägen an. Bettina Speckner verwendet Fotografien, die ihre Mutter während ihres ersten Amerikabesuches gemacht hat, und erinnert damit an Madeleine Albrights Reisen in andere Länder. Hilde De Deckers Münzen aus verschiedenen Ländern hängen an einem Ast wie Kirschen, die darauf warten, gepflückt zu werden, wenn die Außenministerin diese Regionen betritt. Während sie auf den Ozean schaute, dachte Sondra Sherman, daß wie Kontinente geformte Goldfragmente im Wasser treiben könnten und uns daran erinnern, daß der "Globus ein riesiger Edelstein ist". Dieser Gedanke führte zu ihrem Schmuckstück *Continental Drift*. Richard Mawdleys versteinerter, insektenartiger Turm stellt einen Kontrapunkt zu Margareth Sandstöms goldenem Engel dar, der die Außenministerin zu jeder Begebenheit kultiviert zieren könnte. Tore Svensson hofft, daß sie die Gelegenheit finden wird, eine seiner vier Broschen zu tragen, deren Gestaltung von der Trauerkleidung der peruanischen Paracas Indianer abgeleitet ist.

Keine Ausstellung kann ohne die Hilfe einer Gemeinschaft stattfinden. Diese Ausstellung und der Katalog sind durch die Bemühungen vieler Einzelpersonen ermöglicht worden. Die enthusiastische Resonanz der Künstler ließ das ursprüngliche Konzept Wirklichkeit werden, und wir würdigen deren Unterstützung zutiefst. Für ihre Hilfe beim Zusammentragen von Forschungsmaterial möchte ich Martha Flood, der Kustodin unseres Archivs, danken. Ich danke Alexandra Kudrjavcev-DeMilner für ihre Unterstützung beim Zusammenstellen der Biographien mitten in der Arbeit an einem anderen Projekt und Brenda Moore, meiner Galerieassistentin, die in der Endphase dieses Projektes unermeßliche Hilfe geleistet hat. Für die fotografische Dokumentation sorgte Jack Ramsdale unter zusätzlicher Mitarbeit von Thomas Brummett und Joseph Painter. Ein besonderer Dank gilt Michael Lemonick vom *Time Magazine*, der den Kontakt zu Timothy Greenfield-Sanders herstellte und es uns ermöglichte, dessen hervorragendes Portrait von Madeleine K. Albright zu veröffentlichen. Peter Grollman, ein Assistent des US-Senators Arlen Specter war das enthusiastische Bindeglied zwischen unserem Projekt und dem Außenministerium. Wendy Steiner, die sich gerade mit dem Bereich Frauen, Schmuck und Schönheit befaßt, steuerte erfreut einen Essay bei, der die Rolle von Schmuck im Leben einer mächtigen Frau beleuchtet.

1906 schuf René Lalique eine Olivenzweigbrosche mit acht Vögeln, die anfänglich als Tauben gedeutet wurden. Das Schmuckstück war ein symbolisches Geschenk der Bürger von Paris an Mrs. Woodrow Wilson aus Anlaß des Waffenstillstands von 1918, wobei sich die "Tauben" in Friedenstauben verwandelten. Leider blieb diese wohlmeinende Friedensgeste erfolglos, da der Kongreß den Eintritt der USA in den Völkerbund ablehnte und es dadurch verhinderte, dessen Ziele durchzusetzen. Wir können nur hoffen, daß die Symbole, die Madeleine Albright trägt, nicht ebenso fruchtlos bleiben, sondern ihr helfen, in der Welt Harmonie zu stiften, wenn sie auf die Regierungen aller Nationen zugeht. *Brooching It Diplomatically* hebt die Tatsache hervor, daß von Künstlern geschaffener Schmuck über die Grenzen des Schmuckstücks hinausgehen kann und damit größere ästhetische und politische Bedürfnisse erfüllt. Somit feiert diese Ausstellung die angesehene Position der amerikanischen Außenministerin, in deren Persönlichkeit kreative und diplomatische Ausdruckskraft vereint sind.

WENDY STEINER

Brooching Power

Die Ausstellung begann mit einer einfachen Einladung. "Lieber Künstler," schrieb Helen W. Drutt English, "sollen wir das Thema diplomatisch anschneiden?"[1] Es ging um Madeleine K. Albright, die erste weibliche Außenministerin in der amerikanischen Geschichte, und das Wortspiel zu 'brooch' war passender als die Briefschreiberin vermuten konnte. Nach dem Oxford English Dictionary handelt es sich bei 'brooch' und 'broach' um das gleiche Wort, wobei die unterschiedlichen Bedeutungen erst in jüngerer Zeit mit unterschiedlichen Schreibweisen differenziert wurden. 'Brooch' läßt sich auf ein Verb zurückführen, das einstechen, niederstechen, durchstechen bedeutet, in etwas hineinstechen, um jemanden oder etwas zu befreien, anstechen, einer Sache Ausdruck oder Publicity verleihen, eine Konversation beginnen oder über etwas diskutieren, etwas einführen, vorbringen. Etymologisch gesprochen, schneiden Broschen tatsächlich etwas an.

Die Ministerin Madeleine Albright hat diese semantische Übereinstimmung zu ihrem diplomatischen Vorteil eingesetzt. Seit sie diesen höchsten Kabinettsposten angetreten hat, benutzt sie ihre Broschen, um die Ziele ihrer Verhandlungen auszudrücken. Während der vor kurzem abgehaltenen Nahostfriedensgespräche prangte eine Taube auf ihrer Schulter und wurde über die Medien zu allen Beobachtern rund um die Welt getragen. Da dieses symbolische Ausdrucksmittel von männlichen Diplomaten nicht eingesetzt wird, haben Madeleine Albrights juwelenbesetzte Broschen eine öffentliche Diskussion über die Verbindung zwischen Weiblichkeit und Macht ausgelöst. *Time*, *Vogue*, *George* und andere Albright-Beobachter haben die von der Außenministerin erfundene ornamentale Semiotik dokumentarisch festgehalten. Sie trägt eine juwelenbesetzte Spinne, wenn sie sich anmutig fühlt, eine Brosche mit dem Kapitol, um zu zeigen, daß sie für beide Parteien steht, eine Nadel mit einem Ballon, wenn sie in Hochstimmung ist.[2] Wenn sie ihre Bienenbrosche trägt, macht sie sich

Mohammad Alis Rat zu eigen, wie "ein Schmetterling zu schweben und wie eine Biene zu stechen". Sie hat die Biene und nicht den Schmetterling gewählt – eine Botschaft, die ihren Verhandlungspartnern nicht entgeht – aber sie vermittelt sie auf eine Art und Weise, wie sie nur Frauen möglich ist. Wie Ophelias Sprache der Blumen, so drückt die Sprache der Broschen die mentale Einstellung der Außenministerin aus. Sie witzelt: "Deutet meine Anstecknadeln".[3]

Die Broschen der Außenministerin enthüllten manchmal ein Tauziehen zwischen den Deutungen, die andere ihr geben, und denen, die sie für sich gewählt hat. Nachdem die irakische Presse sie eine Schlange genannt hatte, trug sie bei einem Treffen mit Tariq Aziz eine Schlangenbrosche. Als Ratko Mladic eine Ziege nach ihr benannte, schenkte ihr ein amerikanischer Admiral eine Ziegenbrosche. Seine diplomatische Galanterie wandelte eine Beleidigung in ein Kompliment, genauso wie die Schlangenbrosche, die sie in Aziz' Gegenwart zur Schau gestellt hatte. So wie in Shakespeares *Sturm* Kleinodien den Tod versöhnen – "Das sind die Perlen, sie waren seine Augen. Schau!" – tilgen in diesem Fall Broschen Aggressionen und werfen sie zurück auf den Aggressor. Sowohl Madeleine Albright als auch der Admiral zeigen, daß es nicht nur unfein ist, eine Dame zu beleidigen, sondern auch, daß man sich dadurch nur selbst schadet. "Das sind die Perlen, sie waren seine Zurechtweisung. Schau!"

Natürlich haben Künstler seit jeher Schmuck für mächtige Frauen geschaffen. Seien es die Kronjuwelen Englands oder Fouquets Jugendstil-Brustplatten für Sarah Bernhardt, es waren die traditionellen Funktionen des Schmucks, die das Bündnis zwischen Weiblichkeit und Macht unterstützten. Die Kostspieligkeit edler Materialien zeigt das Prestige der Trägerin, die Schönheit der Gestaltung und Ausführung bekräftigt deren Anziehungskraft. Obwohl Monarchinnen grundsätzlich einen komplizierten Weg in der Ausübung ihrer Macht zu beschreiten hatten, so waren die Künste der Darstellung immer ihre Verbündeten. Und was Berühmtheiten und Schauspielerinnen wie Sarah Bernhardt anbetrifft, so hat das Mystische, welches durch den Schmuck entfacht wird, ihre Macht im Bild der Öffentlichkeit verstärkt.

In einer Demokratie, insbesondere in einer post-feministischen Demokratie, können Frauen an den Schalthebeln der Macht jedoch nicht so offen ihre Schönheit, ihren Reiz, ihren Reichtum und ihren Geschmack zur Schau stellen. Im Gegenteil, demokratische Macht muß verteilt erscheinen und nicht konzentriert auf einen überdeterminierten Mittelpunkt. Daher ist in keiner anderen amerikanischen Stadt die weibliche Garderobe so konservativ wie in Washington, wo gesprayte Hochfrisuren als "Machthelme" bekannt sind und wo Erfolgskleidung für eine Frau feuerwehrrote Anzüge mit Goldknöpfen bedeutet. Der Schmuck in Washington drückt anerkannte Werte wie Patriotismus und zurückhaltenden Geschmack aus, und es ist am sichersten, wenn er in Kopien erscheint, die "Jedermann" trägt, wie z.b. der "Freiheitsadler", der noch bis vor kurzem praktisch von jeder First Lady und Politikerin im Land getragen wurde. Der Stil des Kapitols ist eine Angelegenheit der Kontrolle und Konformität, nicht der eigenen Note. Obwohl Frauen ihre Weiblichkeit nicht hinter einer Imitation des Männlichen verstecken sollen, dürfen sie sie auch nicht in einer weiblich-aristokratischen Botschaft ausdrücken, die demokratischer Macht widerspricht – wie Launenhaftigkeit, Eigensinnigkeit, Verlockung, Narzißmus oder unwiderstehlicher Faszination. Sicherlich vermitteln einige Frauen in Washington all diese Botschaften von weiblicher Macht, aber eine Außenministerin könnte dies als problematisch empfinden. Madeleine Albrights Presse zufolge wird das Gleichgewicht zwischen ihrer Weiblichkeit und ihrer Macht kontinuierlich neu ausgehandelt.

Die Broschen dieser Ausstellung spiegeln diese ideologische Vielschichtigkeit wider und enthüllen dabei immerwährende Spannungen in der Schmuckkunst. Ist es das Ziel einer Brosche, die äußere Erscheinung der Trägerin zu steigern, oder sollte sie als eigenständiges Kunstwerk dastehen? Falls eine Brosche eine politische Aussage des Künstlers überbringt, darf dann eine Person des öffentlichen Lebens ihren Körper für diese Botschaft zur Verfügung stellen? Falls das Tragen bedeutet, daß sie sich der Aussage der Brosche anschließt, welchen Einblick hat der Künstler in die Botschaften, die sie vielleicht vermitteln möchte? Ist es für eine Person des öffentlichen Lebens angemessen, Schmuck in einer konventionell femininen Weise einzusetzen, um ihren eigenen Geschmack oder etwa den Wunsch, jemandem zu gefallen, auszudrücken? Oder muß sie sich aller persönlichen Meinungen enthalten und dabei niemals ein Mittel auslassen, um die Würde ihrer Stellung und die Ziele ihrer Mission auszudrücken?

Die Antworten auf diese Fragen sind so vielfältig wie die Künstler dieser Ausstellung. Einige haben sich entschieden, Madeleine Albrights Geschlecht zu ignorieren (nur bis zu einem gewissen Grad, da die Brosche heutzutage konventionell weiblicher Schmuck ist). Frei also, um rein diplomatische Ideen zu vermitteln, drückt Kai Chans *Mountains and Seas* eine Wechselwirkung zwischen Kanada und den Vereinigten Staaten aus, indem sich seine roten Berge in den blauen Wellen auf der anderen Seite der "Grenze" widerspiegeln. Margaret Wests *Cloud Rose* aus weißem, durchscheinendem Marmor fängt eine australische Erhabenheit der Natur ein. Ihr Landsmann Robert Baines verwandelt in seiner roten, filigranen Brosche *Oz Brooch* Känguruhs in wunderliche Designelemente. Jiří Šibor und Pavel Opočenský meißeln amerikanische Symbole in dekorativen Stein: Šibor eine aus Koralle gefertigte Reliefkarte der Staaten mit separaten Korallensteckern für Alaska und Hawaii und Opočenský die amerikanischen Flagge in polierte Jade mit rauhen Kanten, so als ob die Flagge sich im Wind blähte. Diese nationalistischen Symbole – seien sie ernst, lyrisch oder humorvoll – setzen die Außenministerin nur geringem Druck aus, sowohl in ihrer Rolle als Frau als auch als Diplomatin. Sie akzeptieren die Idee der Staatsfrau als unproblematisch.

Wendy Ramshaws und Juhani Heikkiläs Stücke gehen sogar noch weiter in dieser Außerachtlassung des Geschlechts. Ramshaws *Lightning*, ein elektrischer Blitzstrahl aus Silber, Gold und Schmucksteinen, drückt Stärke und geistige Energie aus. "Ich denke, dies ist ein angemessenes Stück für jemanden, der von Logik und Erkenntnisblitzen abhängig ist", schreibt Ramshaw in einem Brief an Helen Drutt.[4] Weiter schreibt sie: "Der 'Blitz' könnte auch als Blitzableiter und Kanal für rationales Denken fungieren. Er ist Ausdruck für ein Moment der Energie."[5] Heikkiläs *Brooch* liefert geradezu eine Begründung dafür, das Geschlecht einer Führungspersönlichkeit zu ignorieren. Es handelt sich um einen nackten Mann mit einem als Arm ausgefahrenen Stab, der die Inschrift "homo communicans" trägt. Wie Latein eine universelle, internationale Sprache ist (oder für Europa einst war), so steht "homo" artgemäß für "Person" – männlich wie dieser Nackte jedoch nur durch die Konvention. Das Wesen der Außenministerin ist das eines Kommunikators, und für Heikkilä ist diese diplomatische Funktion unabhängig von ihrem Geschlecht. Sowohl Ramshaw als auch

Heikkilä postulieren eine post-sexistische Welt, in der Aufgaben von Menschen gut erfüllt werden, wo nicht-geschlechtsspezifische Eigenschaften, in diesem Falle Energie, Logik, intuitive Erkenntnis und Kommunikationsgeschick, wichtig sind.

Auch wenn Künstler Madeleine Albrights Geschlecht nicht ignorieren können, so stellen sie es oft nicht so dar, als ob es irgendeine besondere Auswirkung auf ihre Rolle als Kopf der amerikanischen Außenpolitik hätte. Kiff Slemmons Brosche sieht wie eine Lorgnette mit zwei "Linsen" aus, die Schiffskompassen ähneln. Eine beinhaltet eine Frauenfigur mit einer fließenden Robe, die andere das Silber, das beim Ausschneiden aus der Platte übrig geblieben ist: einmal ist die Frau anwesend, das andere Mal abwesend. Madeleine Albright reist bekanntlich viel, und die amerikanische Inschrift "In God We Trust" vermittelt die Idee, daß sie manchmal im Land ist und zu anderen Zeiten nicht. Die "Kompasse" sind mit einem Plexiglasstab verbunden, auf dessen Spitze eine feine Schreibfeder sitzt. Diese Brosche stellt in einem formal eleganten Design eine Beziehung zwischen Weiblichkeit, offizieller Unterschrift, der Steuermannskunst und dem Reisen her.

Viele Künstler dieser Ausstellung haben die Freiheitsstatue in Beschlag genommen, eine seit langem gültige Darstellung der Vereinigten Staaten als Frau. Marjorie Schicks *Liberty Torch* gibt das berühmte Symbol als einen Strauß von Blumenflammen aus Papiermaché wieder. Betsy King benutzt die Statue in ihrem *World Peace*, welches ein Wortspiel auf die Brosche selbst sein könnte, ein "world piece".[6] Der brillante Gijs Bakker setzt Uhren anstatt der Augen in einen Silberumriß von *Lady Liberty's* Kopf: "Eine Uhr umgekehrt eingesetzt, damit Frau Albright weiß, wie lange ihre Verabredung dauern wird, und eine für den Besucher, damit dieser weiß, wann er zu gehen hat."[7] Bakkers Brosche ist so eine Hilfe für die praktisch veranlagte Madeleine Albright. Mit ähnlicher Aufmerksamkeit stattet Gerd Rothmanns Brosche sie mit einem praktischen Geschenk für besondere Besucher aus. Es handelt sich um eine Plakette mit dem Daumenabdruck der Ministerin und der Inschrift "With Honor and Gratitude, Presented by the Secretary of State Madeleine K. Albright". Die Brosche ruht in einem passenden Etui, in dem Platz für den Namen der Empfängerin gelassen wurde. In ihrem Bemühen um ideologische Botschaften ignorieren einige Künstler Madeleine

Albright. Wie dem auch sei, wie oft hat man schon Gelegenheit, seine Überzeugung an die Schultern eines amerikanischen Außenministers zu heften? Die vom holländischen Künstler Robert Smit angefertigte *Pentagon-Windmill* ist ein exquisites Stück Goldschmiedekunst. Gleichzeitig weist sie aber darauf hin, daß die Schwerter des Pentagon in das holländische Äquivalent der "Pflugscharen", nämlich in Windmühlen, eingeschmolzen werden sollten. Der Schweizer Bernhard Schobinger überkreuzt verrostete Schlüssel auf einem Gefängnisschloß und betont damit den unterdrückenden Charakter politischer Macht. Die afro-amerikanische Künstlerin Joyce Scott knüpft aus Perlenschnüren eine Black Power-Faust, die sie über eine Landkarte von Afrika legt, wobei die rot-weiß-blauen Perlenschnüre für Südafrika stehen; das Ganze nennt sie *Liberty*. Der Franko-Australier Pierre Cavalan schafft "Schmuck" aus Collagen, die wie militärische Orden aussehen: von einer Black Power-Faust gehaltene Bumerange sind an das Abbild australischer Ureinwohner mit Lendenschurz gekettet. Dies impliziert, daß sich von der Situation der Speere tragenden "Eingeborenen" bis zu der der revolutionären Afro-Amerikaner wenig getan hat. Für Cavalan haben beide Länder vieles gemeinsam, vielleicht nicht immer zu ihrem Besten.

Die Aussagen anderer Broschen betreffen nicht nur die Politik, sondern auch die Kunst. Die ausgezeichnete Arbeit von Manfred Bischoff zeigt das surreale Bild einer Gesellschaftsklasse mit der Arbeit *Workingman Hero*. Ein Schädel "schiebt" eine Schubkarre, in der sein kopfloser Körper liegt, dessen "eiserne" Hand im Triumph eine Waffe erhebt. In dieser absurden Allegorie ist der Sieg des Arbeiters auch gleichzeitig sein Verderben, was durch die komplexe Arbeit des Meistergoldschmiedes vermittelt wird. Stephan Seyffert zeigt sich mit seinem Goldbarren, auf dessen Oberseite die Worte "ARTICLE OF VALUE" (Wertgegenstand) eingraviert sind, offener in seiner Kunstideologie. Ist es lediglich das Material der Goldschmiedekunst – in diesem Fall Gold – das wertvoll ist, oder ist es die Arbeit, die der Künstler mit dem Material anfertigt – die Umformung des Materials in ein Symbol seiner selbst, den Goldbarren? Oder sollen wir diese Brosche als ein Wortspiel auf "article of faith" (Glaubensartikel) oder gar "Articles of the Constitution" (Verfassungsartikel) lesen, was heute in der amerikanischen Diplomatie durch einen reinen kommerziellen "article" (hier: Gegenstand) ersetzt wird? Die Israelin Deganit Schocken ist optimistischer, was die Beziehungen zwischen Kunst und Politik angeht. Sie stellt aufrechte grüne Bäume, einen versunkenen See und eine grenzüberschreitende Barriere in einer ausgewogenen Komposition zusammen, um darauf hinzuweisen, daß "trennende Elemente ihren Ort in gegenseitiger Beziehung finden und in einer gemeinsamen Geographie verschmelzen. Integrität hängt von der Einstellung ab, die sich um Harmonie, Schönheit und Frieden bemüht. Wir im Nahen Osten teilen uns Olivenbäume und Sand. Wir müssen unsere Unterschiede ausgleichen."

Für andere Künstler jedoch ist die Möglichkeit, Botschaften durch Schmuck zu übermitteln, nicht so klar. Die beiden Broschen Beppe Kesslers sind dekorative Abstraktionen aus Plexiglas, Stoff, Farbe und Zeitungspapier, in die ein rundes Vergrößerungsglas eingelegt ist. Wenn wir durch die Glasblasen schauen, können wir Fetzen einer Botschaft lesen: "most inspired by the observed (obscene?) local…" und "-d a chance/ want to say/ -ns on whatever/ about/ It is good/ bad". So sehr wir uns auch anstrengen, diese Mitteilung ist schwer zu entziffern – ein Geheimnis (ein diplomatisches? ein persönliches?), das einer wertvollen Oberfläche hinterlegt ist.

Einige Arbeiten dieser Ausstellung versorgen Madeleine Albright mit ausgezeichneter Schmuckkunst. Die geometrische Eleganz von Peter Skubics Entwürfen aus schimmerndem Gold lassen Luxus, Geschmack und ästhetische Tiefe erkennen. Skubic erinnert uns daran, daß das griechische Wort "Kosmos" nicht nur Ordnung (die Welt als geordnetes Ganzes) und Weltraum bedeutet, sondern auch Schmuck und Zier. "Meine Philosophie besteht darin, die Beziehung zwischen diesen verschiedenen Bedeutungen zu finden".[8] Breon O'Caseys Taube fliegt in einem silbernen, sonnengepunkteten Rahmen – eine Komposition, die den keltischen Symbolismus von O'Caseys Wahlheimat Cornwall aufgreift und vom lockeren Zusammentreffen zwischen Landschaft und Abstraktion der St. Ives-Künstler lebt. Auf den letzten, für diese Ausstellung gefertigten Arbeiten des verstorbenen Max Fröhlich spulen sich Golddrähte auf goldenen Rechtecken auf. "Ich frage mich, was Sie von der Idee der Spirale als Symbol für eine hochkarätige Persönlichkeit in dieser Stellung halten", fragte er Helen Drutt in einem Brief. In einer anderen feinen Arbeit wird Lucy Sarneels See-Ear – eine Brosche mit Pflanzenformen aus Zink – in eine verzinkte Scharnierbox eingepackt. Man öffnet den Deckel, so als ob man unter Wasser schauen würde, um einen Blick auf das wimmelnde Leben auf dem Meeresboden zu erhaschen. Eine weitere Einheit zwischen Schmuck und Behälter stellt Catherine Martins Goldarabeske mit ihrer dazugehörigen Box dar. William Harpers *Shiva's Golden Shaft*, Helen Shirks Seeanemonen, Arline Fischs *Ruffled Banner,* Debra Rapoports *Grace* und Detlef Thomas' *Malachite* sind andere Arbeiten, die die reinste Sprache des Schmucks sprechen und damit die Anziehungskraft und das Prestige der Trägerin durch ihre konzentrierte Schönheit vergrößern.

Obwohl viele dieser Broschen von Politik sprechen oder Weiblichkeit ausdrücken, beziehen sich einige auch auf die Beeinflussung der Weiblichkeit durch die Politik. Unter den Elegantesten finden sich Georg Doblers Umsetzungen der "boutonnière" des männlichen Diplomaten in das perfekte weibliche Gegenstück: zwei exquisite Anstecknadeln in Form von Blumen, die eine aus Amethyst und Silber, die andere aus Amethyst und Gold. Auch Ruudt Peters *David* gelingt es, das Weibliche mit dem Männlichen zu verbinden, indem er eine "Antenne" aus Technologie-Draht an einem natürlich gewachsenen Jadekristall befestigt. Peters stellt sich Madeleine Albright vor, wie sie diese Brosche in Gesprächen mit dem israelischen Premierminister Netanyahu trägt, und man fragt sich in diesem Fall, welchen Weg die Symbolik nehmen wird. Wird Israel den jugendlichen David gegenüber dem Goliath der Weltmacht Amerika spielen, oder ist es die Außenministerin, die ihre Courage gegenüber dem angriffslustigen Premierminister auffahren muß?

Mehrere Schmuckkünstler sehen in der Weiblichkeit einen besonderen Nutzen für die Politik. Joan Binkleys Brosche aus Silberperlen ähnelt einem Spiegel, der an das Haupt der Medusa erinnert, auf einem "Griff" in Form eines Skorpionschwanzes – eine Mischung aus traditionellen Zeichen des Narzißmus und der Bedrohung der Frau. Daneben hat Binkley ein Friedenssymbol aus Stahl in den Perlenteilen am unteren Ende der Anstecknadel eingearbeitet, so als ob sie damit implizit sagen wollte, daß Schönheit, Weiblichkeit und Fetisch für die Sache des Friedens eingesetzt werden sollten. Ähnlich nutzen Sharon Churchs *Speak Softly* und *Scatter Pins* Bilder der weiblichen Fruchtbarkeit und Großzügigkeit (die aufbrechende Samenschote und die Hand, die Früchte fallen läßt), um das Gute aufzuzeigen, das von einer mächtigen Frau ausgehen kann. Ihr Titel *Speak Softly* spielt auf das politische Diktum an "Spreche leise und trage einen großen Stock bei dir". Karl Fritschs Anstecknadel ist ein kleines, schwarzes Kätzchen, geschmückt mit zwei Goldkugeln (Brüste? die Perlen einer Kette?). Die Liebenswürdigkeit und die Miniaturisierung dieses Bildes drücken Fritschs anti-monumentale Haltung aus, ein Protest gegen die idealisierte Erhabenheit und aggressive physische Größe deutscher Kunst, die er mit dem Aufkommen des Nationalsozialismus assoziiert.[9] Die winzige Katze setzt Macht ein, indem sie sie in einer "Strategie der Demokratisierung" unterminiert.

Unter den "Aufnahmen" der Kunst der weiblichen Staatsführung überwiegen Humor und Ironie. Peter Chang stattet einen rot-weiß-blauen Spiegel mit Entenfüßen aus – weil "eine Ente vielleicht jemandes Mutter sein könnte"? Sandra Enterline legt eine wirkliche "Bienenkönigin" in einen goldenen Behälter. Judy Onofrio parodiert einen militärischen Orden durch aufgelesene "Juwelen", die um die Kitschbüste eines Hirsches versammelt sind, der grüne Lidschatten und purpurnen Lippenstift trägt. Den Hirschkopf umgeben ein Schlüsselanhänger mit dem Blick auf Mount Rushmore, ein amerikanischer Adler aus Kristallglas und eine glitzernde amerikanische Flagge: All Bright for Madeleine? (Alles klar für Madeleine?) Bruce Metcalfs kleiner, goldener Mann mit einem Ahornblatt als Kopf und einem winzigen Penis zwischen den Beinen trägt eine Holzkiste mit Ahornsamen. Es ist kaum vorstellbar, was es für eine Außenministerin bedeutet, eine solche Brosche zu tragen, besonders da, wie Metcalf bemerkt, "der menschliche Körper sicherlich die intimste und subversivste Arena für Kunstwerke ist".[10] Wenn man aber den Witz dieser ausgezeichneten Karikatur bedenkt, könnte es einfach bedeuten, daß Madeleine Albright mit dem Tragen dieser Brosche ihren Sinn für Humor beweist.

Betsy Kings *Earth Angel* präsentiert eine Reihe von Frauenbildern, denen Madeleine Albright auf ihren Reisen begegnen könnte: ein Engel und eine tauchende Popdiva mit Rasterpunkten und getupftem Bikini. Eingezwängt zwischen den Klischees der Reisemagazine, wie dem Eiffelturm und einer Pyramide, sind eine filigrane Krone und ein florales Muster auf Gold eingearbeitet: elegante, aristokratische Symbole der

Weiblichkeit. Madeleine Albrights Geschlecht wird in den verschiedenen Ländern, die sie besucht, unterschiedlich bewertet, und die Brosche setzt zuvorkommenderweise diese Bedeutungen zu ihrer Information zusammen.

Robin Kranitzky und Kim Overstreet sind gleichermaßen besorgt um das, was Ministerin Albright über sich selbst, und um das, was die Welt über sie denkt. *Profile of a Woman* gewährt einen Einblick in die toupierte Hochfrisur einer Dame mit Lorbeerkranz und einer Rüsche mit den stars and stripes um ihren Ausschnitt. In ihrem Haar finden sich Schnipsel eines Zeitungsportraits der Ministerin: "Ein Leben, in dem nichts dem Zufall überlassen bleibt ... hohe Maßstäbe in Puncto Exzellenz, Integrität und Disziplin ... ernannt von Clinton ... erste Außenministerin ... wuchs in vier Ländern auf ... spricht fünf Sprachen ... höchstrangiges Kabinettsmitglied". Die Zitate setzen sich fort mit "Schwebe wie ein Schmetterling, steche wie eine Biene". Unter der Hochfrisur aber präsentieren Overstreet und Kranitzky die Inhalte dieser "komplexen Identität". Frau Albrights Gehirn bringt die ganze Welt in Verbindung mit dem Kapitol und schließt Sterne, Vögel und Menschen mit ein.

Bussi Buhs' Broschen stellen vielleicht die höchste Herausforderung an Madeleine Albrights Humor dar. Ihr *Shoulder Piece* ist eine aus fleischfarbenen Plastikbrüsten gefertigte Epaulette mit chromgelben Aureolen und orangefarbenen Brustwarzen. Das Schulterstück ist eine vertauschte "Brustplatte", die nackten Brüste bilden infolgedessen das Schulterpolster einer kraftvollen Garderobe. Eine mächtige Frau darf ihre Weiblichkeit als Rüstung einsetzen, wobei ihre Brüste sich wie Stacheln sträuben und sie so stärken. In ihrer Person als politische Kriegerin fungiert ihre Weiblichkeit als ein Bestandteil ihres Waffenarsenals. Sie trägt sie und setzt sie ein. Das Stück ist eine feine Stilisierung, wenn auch aus Plastik – farbenfroh, feingliedrig und gut konturiert. Es sagt aber auch aus, daß eine Kriegerin etwas unweigerlich Komisches an sich hat, und besonders eine, die ein solches Stück auf ihrer Schulter trägt.

Noch grotesker ist Buhs' *Ceremonial Beard*: ein Bart aus Latex, der an Uncle Sams weißen Spitzbart erinnert, den man mit Gazebändern an einem billigen metallenen Kopfband befestigt. Die seltsame Idee dazu kam Buhs, als sie in ihrem Garten ein riesiges Unkraut entfernte, um zu verhindern, daß es seine Samen verstreut. Als sie die

Pflanze untersuchte, konnte sie das Hypokotyl nicht finden: den Punkt, wo die Wurzel beginnt und der Stamm endet, wo die Pflanze nach oben sprießt und nach unten wurzelt. Sie goß Gummi in den hohlen Stamm, um dieses Dilemma aufzuzeigen, und kam zu der Überzeugung, daß "die Parallelen zur Politik leicht zu finden seien".[11] Amerika ist das riesige Unkraut, dessen Samen sie unter Kontrolle bringen möchte und dessen rationaler Standpunkt des "alles in Ordnung – nichts in Ordnung" genauso schwer aufzuzeigen ist wie das Hypokotyl des Unkrautes. Das Innere des hohlen Riesen wird zum grotesken Bart für die Trägerin. Durch die Verkörperung von Uncle Sam in diesem geschlechtsverdrehenden Ausstellungsstück würde die Ministerin sicherlich den sich ausbreitenden Einfluß des Riesen behindern.

Die "Untersuchungen" über die Außenministerin, die in dieser Ausstellung betrieben werden, hätten in keinem anderen Medium dieselben Erkenntnisse zutage gefördert. Denn zumindest in den USA bilden Broschen ein größtenteils weibliches Symbolsystem. Sie geben Materialien, die an sich Werte darstellen, eine Bedeutung – die Kostbarkeit von Gold und Edelsteinen, die sozialen Werte von Prestige, Schönheit und Geschmack. Frau Albright erkennt in Broschen das Zusammenfließen von Faktoren, die ihre Position in der Welt bestimmen, und sie hat sie benutzt, um ihre Ziele voranzubringen. Die Ausstellung erweitert dieses Verständnis um die Kreativität der verschiedenen internationalen Künstler.

[1] "Dear Artist, shall we 'brooch' (broach) the subject diplomatically?" Das Zitat spielt mit den Worten 'brooch' (= Brosche) und 'broach' (= ein Thema anschneiden)
[2] Alain L. Sanders: "Brooching the Subject Diplomatically". In: *Time*, 24.3.1997, S. 36
[3] Steven Erlanger: "A Diplomat Who Says 'Read My Pins'". In: *New York Times*, "Week in Review", 24.5.1998, S. 2
[4] Brief an Helen Drutt, 19.1.1998
[5] ebd.
[6] Weltstück: im Englischen sind 'peace' und 'piece' Homophone
[7] Brief an Helen Drutt, 11.12.1997
[8] Peter Dormers Text in: Helen Drutt English und Peter Dormer: *Jewelry of Our Time: Art, Ornament and Obsession*. New York 1995, S. 184
[9] Susanne Gaensheimer: "Anti-monumentality: Strategies of Democratization in Contemporary German Art". In: *Index. Contemporary Art and Culture*, 3.4.1997, S. 40–44 und 91–93
[10] Peter Dormer und Ralph Turner: *The New Jewelry: Trends and Tradition*. London 1994 (neue, überarbeitete Auflage), S. 184
[11] Brief an Helen Drutt, 27.10.1997